ALTERED STATE

A **Guardian Book**

ALTERED STATE

SOUTH AFRICA 1990

DAVID BERESFORD
MICHAEL BILLINGTON
BREYTEN BREYTENBACH
ALEX BRUMMER
GEORGINA HENRY
ANGELLA JOHNSON
FRANK KEATING

NOMAVENDA MATHIANE
IAN MAYES
DOUGLAS MORRISON
ES`KIA MPHAHLELE
ROGER OMOND
JUDY RUMBOLD
ALAN RUSBRIDGER

HUGO YOUNG

WITH PHOTOGRAPHS BY DON MCPHEE

FOURTH ESTATE · LONDON

First published in Great Britain in 1990 by
Fourth Estate Ltd
289 Westbourne Grove
London W11 2QA

Copyright © 1990 This collection Guardian Newspapers Ltd,
Breyten Breytenbach (Chapter 1), Lionel Abrahams (Chapter 23).

A CIP record for this book is available from the
British Library upon request

ISBN 1-872180-67-1

Printed in Great Britain by Clays Ltd, Bungay, Suffolk

Contents

	Preface *Alan Rusbridger*	7
1	The joy of freedom *Breyten Breytenbach*	*11*
2	Frontiers of a new land *Hugo Young*	*16*
3	Issues of the day *Alan Rusbridger*	*39*
4	Don't get lippy, missy *Angella Johnson*	*44*
5	One for the road *Roger Omond*	*53*
6	Brothers in lore *David Beresford*	*63*
7	Lion in dove's clothing *David Beresford*	*73*
8	The hidden war *Alan Rusbridger*	*82*
9	On patrol *Judy Rumbold*	*89*
10	Behind the wire *Alan Rusbridger*	*93*
11	Learning and losing *Douglas Morrison*	*98*
12	Internal exiles *Douglas Morrison*	*108*
13	Sickness in the system *Angella Johnson*	*112*
14	Pressing for change *Georgina Henry*	*117*

15	Voices on the line *Georgina Henry*	145
16	In black and white *Nomavenda Mathiane*	150
17	Wish you weren't there *Frank Keating*	153
18	Wealth, the front line *Alex Brummer*	157
19	White woman's burden *Judy Rumbold*	179
20	Mothers of a nation *Judy Rumbold*	184
21	Love in the shadows *Judy Rumbold*	189
22	Township Fever *Michael Billington*	197
23	A role for the theatre *Michael Billington*	203
24	Into the skin *Lionel Abrahams*	210
25	Stolen lives *Ian Mayes*	211
26	Sparks of talent *Nadine Gordimer*	221
27	The right to read *Ian Mayes*	224
28	Letter to a young writer *Es'kia Mphahlele*	228
29	Living with a paradox *Liz McGregor*	235
30	A place not on the map *Ian Mayes*	240
31	Accused One and Two *Alan Rusbridger*	248
	Contributors	253
	Acknowledgements	256

Preface

THE MAN from the embassy was distinctly cool about the whole idea. "*Ten* Guardian journalists?" he asked in a tone that suggested that one was one too many. The ambassador, Mr Killen, was still more sceptical. "I am old enough to remember Adam Raphael," he said gravely — an oblique reference to a series on South African wage rates published in the Guardian *circa* 1973. This was back last summer, when FW was still but a twinkle in PW's uncomprehending eye and when the old crocodile was still sharpening his teeth for his last inglorious stand. The embassy was not at all sure Pretoria would like the idea. The Guardian and the South African government had not always, as it were, seen eye to eye.

We sent off the visa forms anyway and wondered where we might go instead. We'd mounted similar expeditions to Belfast, Moscow and Tokyo. Eastern Europe looked the most interesting — just how interesting we didn't guess at the time. We toyed with revisiting Moscow. But the longer we waited for news from Pretoria the more interesting South Africa itself became. By the time FW was installed and began to show his true colours it was positively fascinating.

The aim of the exercise was as before. Take a team of specialists and spread out into a society that is, by and large, unfamiliar to them. Each is there to look at a small part of the bigger picture. Put the bits together at the end and, with luck, you have a panorama where previously you had a microscope or, at best, a telescope. The news that the trip was to be allowed arrived on February 2 — the day of FW's momentous, bridge-burning speech. We decided to wait until the euphoria over Mandela's release had died down before making the journey. We were right to do so, for a visit at that time would have produced an entirely distorted snapshot. One of my own lasting impressions of the trip was dinner with an extremely impressive and thoughtful white businessman in Johannesburg. February 2, he confided, was one of the greatest days of his life — the day he'd always dreamed he'd live to see. With the very next breath he was telling me how he'd recently had a discreet chat with the British embassy in South Africa to see if there weren't some provision for getting himself and his family the hell out of South Africa, together with the appropriate paperwork and work permits.

Of the party, only two of us had been to South Africa before. We made one addition to the original group. Angella Johnson, a Guardian reporter who is black, said she'd like to visit friends in the country. She travelled separately from the main party on a tourist visa.

It should be said that the South African authorities, having decided to let us in, were unfailingly helpful. Most of us went our own way most of the time, and did so freely, but the embassy in London and the information department in Pretoria did their best to open a wide variety of doors. It probably needs adding that, of course, we paid our own way.

THE HOT front page news the day we arrived was not the political negotiations, nor the war in Natal. It was the arrival of final documentary proof that Fanny Bees, the wife of a 19th century mining magnate, was coloured.

The matter of Ms Bees' colour has been contested ever since she appeared, distinctly dusky, in a SABC TV series, Barney Barnato. Ms Bees' descendants were outraged, claiming that Fanny, wife of the flamboyant gold millionaire, was Persil white. Court action was promised. But extensive research by the Bureau for Genealogy at the Human Sciences Research Coucil claims to have proved beyond doubt that Fanny was classified as "a non-white person born at the Cape".

There are many such dark skeletons in South African cupboards, according to Jan van der Merwe, an expert in genealogical exhumations. Indeed, he believes there are between 500,000 and one million Afrikaners whose blood is not quite the colour they imagine it to be. Volk heroes he claims have tainted blood in their veins include Paul Kruger, John Vorster, D F Malan, F W de Klerk and even the Conservative Party (CP) leader Andries Treurnicht.

"I warn clients about the possibilities of turning up non-whites in their family trees, " he says, "but sometimes they still refuse to accept what I find out." The Johannesburg Star noted that the controversy about Ms Bees could happen only in South Africa, adding with uncharacteristic understatement: "Many people here are inclined to be a trifle touchy about these matters."

MEANWHILE FW is shedding friends as fast as he is making them. The testimony of former friends is revealing, if only for emphasising how far FW has travelled in the past six months. Fani Jacobs, a CP MP, has known De Klerk years and shares the same academic legal background. So what does he think of FW now? Professor Jacobs pauses and chooses his words with care. "He's a political crook. He's dishonest. He's not a man of integrity. He's a man who lied to his own. He's a weak man and he's a traitor to his race." In other words, he's not all bad.

Alan Rusbridger
May, 1990

1 The joy of freedom

Breyten Breytenbach

NELSON MANDELA is free! The word rustles like a breeze through the townships, whispered in awe, shouted in triumph from mouth to mouth, from shack to box-house. Did you hear? People wipe their eyes in wonder, greyheads laugh, babies squawk, dust rises from under the feet of young Comrades running the streets with the black, gold and green banner. In the veld small boys with bobbing loincloths whistle shrilly and hurl twirling sticks at recalcitrant beasts. By noon they will take the shade under a thorntree to tell tall tales, each in turn a proud Mandela.

In Qunu of the green hills the clan will be sprucing up the graves of Nosekeni and Henry Gadla Mandela. This is where "Buti" must come to sleep the night and cleanse his hands before the slaughtering of the sacrificial ox. Napilisi, his nephew, says: "All I know is he was put in prison because he wanted equal salary for all." In his wayside store, Makgatho is trying to capture his father's image on the television screen the way one attempts to net a butterfly.

"Nelson Mandela has been released!" Old women lift their skirts to step up to the memory of a youth of rhythm and stomp. The reeds bend with the light. Old men marvel at the trembling of history and drown in thick beer this day, and the hump of accumulated days scarred with the pain of poverty.

On Robben Island, in Pollsmoor and Victor Verster and Zonderwater and Brandvlei and Barberton and Diepkloof and all the other hell-holes of humiliation, prisoners bang their tin plates and chant: "Man-de-la! Man-de-la!" And in the quieter quarters of dehumanisation the politicals stand taller to look the warders straight in the eye. Old guards remember and talk softly to their old wives. Torturers put a finger under a sweaty collar; they are thinking about changing their addresses. Security experts pore over the store of tapes and secret photos with which they hope to blackmail the leader: Mandela with Coetsee, Mandela with Viljoen, Mandela with De Klerk, Mandela laughing with his head thrown back, Mandela relieving himself, Mandela in tears.

Poets are biting their pens. Yuppies, caught in a traffic jam, wind down their windows with a bronzed hand to shout: "Mandela!" Cabinet ministers take medicine and look at one another in distrust. It is hot on the beaches; sun-reddened farmers from the interior squat attentively around portable radios. On the mountain slope above Cape Town harbour "bergies" wipe their stained mouths; one bum reminisces with the toothless grin of timelessness: "I remember the day King George came to town . . ." Burly men in khaki garb snarl insults at their mocking labourers. Behind closed shutters a hit-man thoughtfully oils his rifle. Maybe the earth is heaving, the sea swollen with

THE JOY OF FREEDOM

expectations. Old dreams pour forth. "We have liberated Mandela!" Grown fighters sob. Professionals plot new allegiances. Ancient companions review their splattered lives. "Now the problems start." His wife is working out which dress to wear for what occasion. Go-betweens are offering two minutes, four minutes, three smiles and a nod, dollops of his availability . . . for a price. In Havana, Moscow, Lusaka, London — wherever silence caught up with the exiles — some people will remember to visit the places where the bones of tired strugglers are mouldering in foreign soil, to whisper: "Yes, it's nearly finished now. Soon we shall be going home."

All over the world children wriggle out of their mothers' wombs, screaming at the light, to be named Nelson Rolihlahla Madiba Mandela. In African capitals students wave hand-printed placards defying rot and corruption, and perhaps imperialism too. Miners straighten their backs and wipe their brows. In glittering salons of the Organisation of African Unity, bureaucrats try to get a grip on events as they sip at small cups of coffee and feed the prayer beads in a trickle through their fingers. There are holes in the carpets. Musicians weave the magic mantra of Mandela into their melodies in Wolof and Swahili. Pygmies along their forest tracks, Bedouins in their encampments wrapped up against the winds of the sun, hunters along the flanks of simmering volcanoes — all invent the past and the limitless future stretching all the way to freedom of a man who once lived and who was called Mandela.

"Nelson Mandela is free!" The news reverberates around the globe. Jesse Jackson and Margaret Thatcher and Helmut Kohl and George Bush screech and scratch to get a morsel of the glory. In Warsaw and Berlin and Accra and London the lost and scattered children of South Africa, and some from Azania, the broken warriors expelled from the movements, are getting drunk and obnoxious. In India a fat wrestler changes his name to that of Mandela so as to draw larger crowds to the fairgrounds. In New York a trembling hand writes: "Dear Mister Mendalla, my husband is lamed, we don't need much, I have no one else to turn to . . ."

The powerful of the world issue bloated statements, and confidentially ask their ambassadors: "How long will he last?" On Caribbean islands, in a swirl of rum spat out and cigar smoke, he is incorporated into the Voodoo Pantheon to unite forces with Legba and Victor Hugo and Toussaint Louverture and Baron Samedi. Mummified dreams are being dusted down. In Japan a new doll comes on the market with the features of the world's oldest prisoner. In Peru the Shining Path guerrillas cheer and shake their bitter machetes. In Central Europe, intellectuals ask: "Mandela who?" Somewhere in Cambodia a political commissar gives Mandela to the Khmer Rouge as example and justification. In Western cities young revolutionaries with feverish eyes and death at the throat, shout "Mandela!", hoping that this revolution at least will not be aborted in blood.

Old gulag inmates taste the salt on the wind and sigh, and are bothered by something in the eyes. In poorhouses, in hiding places, in dungeons, in old age homes, people murmur: "So it hasn't been for nothing after all." An impresario is putting together talent for a sing-along. In Korea and Finland they spell his name wrong. On French television, marathon talkers

THE JOY OF FREEDOM

miraculously find a second breath. People swell up with self-satisfied indignation as they use Mandela as a battering ram to get at the adversaries.

Literary agents are sending urgent faxes. Lovers suddenly break down and start sobbing in the hollow of their beloved's shoulders. The night has become small. A Hollywood mogul is hollering instructions down the line to offer him any effing price he wants, as long as it is for ex-clu-si-vi-ty! Multinational bosses reassess strategies and instruct their minions to have advertisements of welcome published immediately. A child writes a birthday card and mails it to Nelsin Mondale, South Africa. Obsequious secretaries silently enter offices to place files on leather-topped tables. Smirking presidential advisors twirl non-existent moustaches.

An old man emerges from prison. He went in an activist, he comes out a myth. He worries about his prostate gland, his notes. A horizon lights up: he brings hope, and he never knew the world, nor the soft caress of empty days under drifting clouds. If he ever did, he no longer remembers. Perhaps there is now a little more sense to our dark passage on earth. He has kept body and soul together with pride and the impossibility of love. He will succeed. He will fail. He lives. He will die. Nelson Mandela is opening a door.

2 *Frontiers of a new land*

Hugo Young

AHMED Kathrada, born of a scholarly Muslim family in the Western Transvaal, spent more than 26 years as a prisoner alongside Nelson Mandela on Robben Island. What strikes you about him, now that he heads the embryonic Department of Information and Publicity in the newly legalised African National Congress is the mildness of his manner and the seriousness of his purpose. He has the calm fluency of an academic, or possibly a country solicitor. But the calm conveys an iron gravitas such as I have met in few democratic politicians anywhere: perhaps because none has suffered so much for the calling Kathrada aspires to. He's as far removed as could ever be from the foaming warrior whom two generations of white South Africans have been taught to associate with the ANC.

I was fortunate he found space for me. One sign of the times in South Africa is that black leaders are a lot harder to see than white. They're always in meetings, usually with each other. They also exist at the point where democrat merges with bureaucrat. No one in the ANC, it seems, may talk to a journalist before consulting with the comrades; a wearisome process, reeking of the old Communist connection, which serves no purpose.

When met, however, the ANC people, young and old, show qualities similar to Kathrada's. They decline to be either surprised or exultant at the position in which they find themselves, talking across the table to their hounders and oppressors of 40 years. The only concession Kathrada makes, and the only smile he wryly gives, concerns the duration of the ecstatic welcome he and the others have received in the free world, and the new privation this has imposed. "I've been able to walk more in Stockholm than Johannesburg", he notes. For the rest, he exhibits a measured certainty that the destiny for which he and thousands of others have suffered hugely is about to come to pass.

Whether he is right, is what the next three or four years of South African history will be about. Most people agree it will take that long for the negotiations begun in early May 1990 to reach agreement — or not. It will be one of the most protracted and intensive parlays of modern times, one of several features that distinguish it from the east European events with which it is falsely compared, as if Presidents Gorbachev and De Klerk formed some neatly symmetrical proof of a better world all round. Before they meet the whites in earnest, or while they're doing so, the blacks have their own problems to face. The newest big party in the world must confront the oldest big problem in the world: and the politics of novelty has its price.

This newness is everywhere. The ANC is not yet even a proper party, still a liberation movement. Its Johannesburg office is so new that Kathrada had difficulty finding me a copy of the Freedom Charter, its basic document. Three crises, in ascending order of importance, cloud the euphoria which attended Mandela's release and the ANC's own unbanning and will perch on the negotiators' shoulders throughout the next four years.

The first, and least, is a crisis of organisation. They were no better prepared than anyone for De Klerk's astonishing *coup de theatre* on February 2, 1990, when he announced what sounded like democracy for South Africa. The ANC reaction was incoherent, and still is. Not surprising, perhaps, for an organisation which, although always committed to political solutions, had been driven by white intransigence into armed struggle, and had perhaps 30,000 of its members in exile or jail. But the problem of adapting to politics is massive. Out of the euphoria must somehow grow branches, structures, lines of democratic accountability. "We don't even know whether it is realisable", says Ahmed Kathrada.

The second crisis, more enduring, is of ideology. Throughout its modern existence, the ANC has been a single-issue organisation, and that issue has not concerned the substance of policy. Dedicated to the task of liberation — a massive undertaking, deployed against immense odds — it has given little time to reaching conclusions, or at any rate agreement, on the kind of society, and especially the kind of economy, it wants the liberated South Africa to look like. But this question has become indistinguishable from liberation itself, for the terms of the deal that must eventually be struck — or not — require an answer from the ANC on what it wants to do with power, or the "power-sharing" De Klerk hopes to confine it to.

Again, sympathy is in order. Who could but quail before the enormity of the task? If, as is supposed to be axiomatic to all sides, majority rule replaces minority tyranny, the votes of some 25 million black citizens will be unleashed against the inheritance of decades, where for example: blacks are still prevented by law, with rare exceptions, from owning land in 87 per cent of the territory; personal income is more unequally distributed than in any other country (the most recently available figure showing that, where white personal income is measured at an index of 100, incomes of Asians, Coloureds and Blacks are respectively 26, 20 and 9); political power at last September's election was won by a party representing 6.3 per cent of the potential electorate; and in this year's Budget, which gives unprecedented handouts to the blacks, social spending continues to be five times greater on whites.

The list of inequities which any ANC ideology must address could be generously extended. The mode of their resolution is far from obvious, and is already giving birth to an extended sub-culture of advisers — composed substantially of white liberal academics who have spent a lifetime pouring scorn on Afrikaner intransigence and doing what little they could to undermine it. In a hundred conferences being spawned world-wide on the future of new South Africa, they're being put rapidly to service.

Meanwhile, the ANC's own first response has caused consternation. On his way out of prison, Mr Mandela talked about nationalisation, of gold mines in particular, as a continuing part of ANC policy. For the whites, socialism has thus been added to racial domination as the spectre to be feared, and supplies a grateful regime with a cause somewhat more righteous than apartheid. "We will not hand over this country to a Socialist Marxist Government", booms the Foreign Minister, Pik Botha. "I do not intend to go to the electorate with a model that will mean suicide", says De Klerk.

A certain naivete, almost certainly not false, attaches to these remarks. Given the scale of the black economic crisis, it would have been incredible if the ANC's first move had been to abandon this cherished expedient. With what other policy would De Klerk address it? Besides, Mandela's speech was therapeutic. South African business had seriously imagined it could oversee political reform without economic change: the opposite illusion to that which exploded in front of the Chinese a year ago. According to the Afrikaner economist, Sampie Terreblanche, a professor at Stellenbosch University, Mandela "shook the Rip van Winkles of the business community out of their sleep and complacency".

All the same, he also raised the question which political reality will oblige the ANC to answer with greater clarity in the next year. Is it a socialist party? Kathrada, once a member of the Communist Party, says it never has been. "We are committed to the mixed economy", he insists. He is echoed by Patrick "Terror" Lekota, publicity secretary of the United Democratic Front, which is not quite co-terminous with the ANC. Lekota, an impressively hard-headed man of 41 with a large future role, says the ANC is "neither capitalist nor socialist". On this issue at least half the chances of success in the negotiations will turn.

Meanwhile, another answer to it exposes the ANC's third looming crisis, and potentially the worst: a crisis of legitimacy. For whom exactly does it speak? So far it is the first participant invited to these talks towards a new country, and has readily assumed mastery. Despite its lack of preparation, seigneurial confidence exudes from its spokesmen. Yet it cannot command the field. If the spluttering effusions of Pik Botha give an impression of the ANC's unmatched militancy, they seriously mislead.

The most emphatic answer to the economic question I heard from a black leader was given by a teacher in the religious studies faculty at the University of Cape Town. The Rev Jerry Mosala is president of Azapo, an umbrella group rooted in Black Consciousness which, while once hoping to form a bridge between the ANC and its historic rival, the Pan-Africanist Congress, now stands outside both of them. Mosala, a mild-mannered man of great civility, educated in Manchester not Moscow, sees the negotiations simply as a trap, and their motive force as having come from international capital.

Blacks, Mosala believes, should not be talking by grace and favour of De Klerk. To do so "discounts the huge sacrifices our people have made to overthrow apartheid completely". The whites want to talk, he argues, merely to stabilise a situation already rigged massively in their favour. Talks ought to await their final crushing, which the struggle would ultimately bring about. To my suggestion that white capital was essential to the future of black South Africa, Mosala was unyielding. The struggle must be recognised. "We may want foreign investment. But we don't want to be held to ransom."

Mosala was the only man I met, who explicitly wanted the De Klerk-Mandela talks to fail. Benny Alexander, the fiery new General Secretary of the PAC — "The PAC are very definitely a socialist party" — while opposing the talks, took the more sinuous line that their failure would be delayed: they might succeed at the table but would collapse on the streets, he said with relish.

These two very different men, it should be added, are, like Mandela himself, fronting organisations that already know a great deal about the bloody politics of the street. The growing number of killings, of blacks by blacks, is not confined to the Natal Zulus of Chief Buthelezi battling to the death with the ANC/UDF. According to John Kane-Berman, director of the Institute of Race Relations, who admittedly sounds like a Buthelezi sympathiser, Natal is now the site of 70 per cent, rather than last year's 90 per cent, of the slaughter. In the Cape Town black townships, according to a British observer, Mosala's people have taken a serious hacking, only stanched when Azapo decided to retaliate.

The stream of murders is a sub-text to the ANC's great project. What goes for Buthelezi's war-lords also goes for the resumption of "necklacing" with burning tyres, which is an ANC trademark. There have been 19 so far this year. Either the leaders cannot stop them, or they decline to do so: the messages are equally worrying, whether from Natal or Soweto. They cast valid doubt, which will deepen, on the mandate to which the ANC lays claim.

That mandate, nevertheless, begins by being irresistibly acted out. The spectacle is impressive, moving and, to many who have lived through the insane years of statutory apartheid, still barely credible. All factions in black South Africa cling to the same dream, which has the power of classic myth: the idea of genuine democratic freedom. Mandela personifies this myth, and no man could be better able to do the job. Even Jerry Mosala, an unfanatical extremist, would like to believe in him: and, at the level of myth personified, does so.

The most appealing element of this myth, amid the myriad problems that surround it, is the part that whites find impossible to understand, because it so signally fails to mirror their own ingrained attitude. An outsider finds it almost as hard to credit, given the history. It consists of the ANC's determined rejection of racialism. It firmly proposes itself as a non-racial party.

When Kathrada says that it has "never called for black majority rule, only for a democratic majority", he is not being a casuist or a hypocrite, but speaking the most profound and moral lesson he has learned from the shattering of his life.

Frank Chikane, general secretary of the South African Council of Churches, offers equally humbling testimony for a man tortured several times in prison, who once had his hair torn out and was forced to collect it from the floor and put it in a dustbin. "I lay my head on the block", Chikane told me. "If the ANC governed the country by oppressing the whites, I would go back to prison."

This is the noble face of African nationalism. It presents two challenges. One, to the whites: can they begin to reciprocate? The second to itself: can a noble purpose receive its pragmatic fulfilment?

WHEN President F W de Klerk met Mrs Thatcher in mid-May, each would have recalled a key moment in the enterprise on which the president is now boldly embarked. It occurred at an earlier meeting, in June 1989, when the Prime Minister read De Klerk the severest of lectures on ending apartheid, releasing Mandela and contemplating some kind of end to white supremacy. I was sceptical of Downing St claims for the crucial importance of this meeting. A week in South Africa showed me its place in the scheme of what has happened — but for a reason Mrs Thatcher will doubtless never acknowledge.

The Thatcher lecture, explaining to De Klerk that she couldn't keep up her anti-sanctions stand for ever, wasn't the first cause of the revolution he may now have unleashed. The internal pressure of demography and economics pointed starkly to a society sustainable only by armed force unless there was some reform, and after years in P W Botha's laager of optimistic fantasy a president exists with courage and intelligence enough to get the message. What he now proposes — universal suffrage in at least one parliamentary chamber — far exceeds anything the British Tories thought reasonable to suggest.

Foreign pressure was also, by universal consent in Cape Town, critical. The American banks can take credit for their tough impositions, and so can the American political system. Here too the message of the figures was inexorable, and supplied the background to Mrs Thatcher's influence. The arch anti-sanctioneer, she would have been entirely negligible if sanctions hadn't existed. That is the answer to her anti-sanctions triumphalism. For her power she depended absolutely on others doing what she pronounced to be futile and immoral. In the interrogation cell, the soft cop with the cigarette only comes into play after the hard one with the knuckleduster.

Still, she played the part. This time the atmosphere at Chequers was bound to be different, not least because the hostess is now reeling and her visitor bestrides his country. Whatever else he will or will not do, he has finally obliterated the ideology of white supremacy. Its doctrinal basis, which has always distinguished South African racism from that of every other regime since Hitler, is gone. Some people are naive enough to think that this automatically means the agreed end of white domination. That's far from certain. But we are left with something rationally intelligible: a naked struggle for power.

Nor is De Klerk's shift as vast a political risk as it looks from London. It has its white constituency. Moving to end apartheid is a relief to a lot of modern Afrikaner politicians, who are now prepared to confess that they've been unhappy with it for years. They've even been hearing awkward moral questions from the Dutch Reformed Church. Clean young men like Roelf Meyer, the deputy minister for constitutional development, and Nick Koornhof, Nationalist Party MP for Swellendam, look you in the eye and sound like American Democrats promising a new frontier for the 1990s.

For the NP, moreover, the price of democracy may be painfully measurable. On the basis of last September's election figures, the party could expect a mere six per cent of a vote by universal suffrage, giving it perhaps 12 seats out of 200. "The first job to go will probably be mine", says Koornhof, "but I am working enthusiastically for the reforms." He claims to have had no word of criticism from his constituents, and many unsolicited statements of gratitude on Cape Town street corners. To Meyer, who will be one of the chief mechanics of the negotiations, the Nats look safer than they did five years ago. "Nothing indicates to me that we have to fear politically", he told me, and I think he meant it.

One does not need prolonged exposure to South African politics to find such talk incredible. How could something so deeply embedded as white supremacy in the politics and economics, not to mention the brain and bone, of Afrikanerdom be thus painlessly excised? It asks us to believe that South Africa will be transformed at a single stroke from the darkest dungeon of undemocracy, not merely into the home of political freedom, but into a place where the master race will surrender a century of privilege without a murmur. South Africa, in other words, is set fair for uniqueness in the annals of world political history.

If this picture is hard to accept as a theoretical proposition, the sceptic will also find support from certain objective realities. Two tendencies in particular argue for bleak caution. South Africa is not unique after all. Listen, first, to the NP's enemies on the Right: and then examine what it really seems to be proposing.

Of the many politicians I met in a week, the one with the most trivial grasp on long-run reality was Dr Andries Treurnicht, leader of the Conservative Party. But Treurnicht is the unmentioned residual of most NP conversations. As the chief remaining exponent of doctrinal racism, he stands to inherit the legacy of breakdown between De Klerk and Nelson Mandela. For if one thing seems certain in this fluid scene, it is that the Nats' future role does depend on a species of success with the ANC. Out of failure will arise Treurnicht's future of dark foreboding, backed by a million men at arms.

As a potential militia leader, Treurnicht cuts an unconvincing figure. An elderly divine of Dutch Reform, he prefaces most remarks with a nervous, high-pitched giggle. His alternative to the Nats' plan carries the lunacies of apartheid to a higher plane, with territorial "homelands" for Coloureds and Indians without territory to match, and a partitioned white state that appears to ignore every lesson apartheid ever taught about the place of black labour in an even half-viable economy. He has persuaded himself that the break-up of the Soviet empire is only the most recent evidence that partition is "a general thing all over the world". "It's just that we didn't have the luck to inherit it", he gnomically adds.

So Treurnicht does not speak for a persuasive reality. He is mad — but he is also bad, in a country where badness may yet appeal to significant numbers of the white constituency who do not find him dangerous to know. He articulates a furious contempt, which an unknown quantity of them will share, for the NP's adoption of policies "which it rejected for so many years". And he has begun to supply them, if they want to listen, with a lurking justification for violent retaliation if they see their birth-right being removed.

Treurnicht is in trouble over violence. The main Afrikaner newspapers, moving into line behind the Government, excoriate him. *Die Burger* expended a lot of venom on his recent caution to supporters not to "jump the gun" when talking of "guns and shooting": a choice of metaphor that seemed to incite even as it affected to restrain. To me, Treurnicht was scarcely more guarded. It was "not up to every individual to grab guns and start shooting", he said. But one could explain their enthusiasm by frustration at not being able to debate or vote on De Klerk's evil impositions. "They are on the sidelines and they want to do something". It was "not impossible" that there would a white uprising which would range his own party against the security authorities: always assuming, as he did not say, that the police can be relied on to come to the aid of De Klerk, despite copious evidence, now that the ANC has ceased to be the enemy, of the trouble some policemen have in deciding where their loyalties lie.

It is impossible at this stage to assess the measure of Treurnicht's threat. This is a constituency that has never faced the test de Klerk is now asking it to pass. One answer the Government gives the sinister doctor is to say, in the words of deputy minister Meyer, that Treurnicht "cannot at the same time lead a parliamentary party and a resistance movement". In the context of South Africa that seems a somewhat refined constitutional nicety. A sounder bulwark may be offered by what the De Klerk team, who put this deal together and have so far carried the NP caucus with them, hope to see coming out of it.

For Treurnicht asks one serious question. It's the same question asked by the ANC. They share, in unholy combination, certain other perspectives, such as the belief that George Bush is pulling the NPs' strings, to which Treurnicht's party adheres as stubbornly as some black nationalists intone their conviction that international capital is behind the whole charade. But the question on which they most closely agree is: what exactly does "power-sharing" mean?

Treurnicht puts it brutally. How can power be shared between a minority and majority, he asks. No way, he replies. The thing's a fraud: which is precisely the conclusion suspected by the ANC. This defines the ground on which the Government is careful to cloak its intentions, perhaps because it does not exactly know them.

De Klerk's formulation is well worked out. He accepts majority rule, but not if it's "simplistic". Although he seems to see that no modification of its simplicity can be based on "ethnic" rights, he insists on protection of "cultural" minorities. These are not word-games but the essential specifics that need to be recognised if the whites are not to commit what the president repeatedly refers to as suicide. Yet are they not a fatal violation of majority rule?

De Klerk and others also say, with a sweep of the arm, that statutory apartheid will soon be entirely liquidated. As our coverage shows, actual apartheid, petty or grand, is far from gone. But the promises about the laws remain to be fulfilled. No-one seems to doubt that separate amenities will go, but the precise changes in Group Areas await legislative form, and fundamental reform of the Land Acts has been specifically ruled out. At any rate, it will happen only after not before negotiation.

This modest start, with little given away, has already done a lot for South Africa's image. Her pariah status is ending. Eighteen heads of state queued to wait upon De Klerk at the Namibian independence celebrations. Foreign politicians are suddenly flooding into Cape Town. If the first purpose of De Klerk's initiative was to capture the high moral ground, there are plenty in the West who are keen to acknowledge that he has done so.

This surprises some people who are closer to the Afrikaner mind. Dr Beyers Naude, an Afrikaner clergyman with a record, for a white man, of unparalleled courage in fighting apartheid, was on the ANC team at the historic round of talks-about-talks. His vision is startlingly optimistic. He sees, in the end, "a great longing by the whites to be accepted by the blacks", he told me. "We will ask how are we to become part of an African country, South Africa." But as for the present, Naude thinks the West have been incautious in their reading of De Klerk. "His statements bear scrutiny. He has not misled anyone, but he has been careful. Unfortunately, the political leadership of the West have bluffed themselves."

The best reinforcement for this reading comes not from the hard Right, whom De Klerk needs somehow to propitiate, but from other liberal Afrikaners, themselves committed to change. Professor Terreblanche believes that the whites have by no means accepted that they will lose power — "and I doubt whether De Klerk has either". Neil van Heerden, the top civil servant in the Department of Foreign Affairs, puts a shape on the nightmare that terrifies them. "We are eager to get back into the world", he said. "But what white fear is really about is downtown Cape Town looking like downtown Accra."

There is no sign that De Klerk is prepared even to contemplate that risk. Even though ministers have said there will never be another all-white election, he has to be able to convince his own voters that it won't happen, or risk catastrophic reprisals from even worse men than the giggling Dr Treurnicht. With the exception of Treurnicht, all the politicians I saw seemed to think they could do it: in other words, that their own guile, percipience and inherited mastery, not to mention the objective facts of economic reality, could in fact, whatever the institutional arrangements, preserve most of life as they knew it. Because that was, was it not, the only way for *all* the people?

WHEN the talks with President De Klerk opened in early May, Nelson Mandela made, as he often has in these times, a statement of prophetic simplicity. Measuring the scale of this great enterprise, he said: "We must deny the past its attempt to enslave us". It was an elemental plea that, in the search for one South Africa, all sides should develop a capacity to forget. But it was also acutely challenging. There can be no doubt that, if this new South Africa is to be born, the blacks must be ready to forget a great deal more than the whites.

The whites, it may be said, have already been prepared to forget a lot. Look at the sacrifices De Klerk has suddenly said that he will make. See the selfless wisdom inherent in his commitment to some version of majority rule, and the risk he now takes to achieve it. Must this remarkable act not be accommodated and at every cost encouraged by outsiders? Is it not, above all, the wielders of power who must be rewarded for preparing to concede it?

I think this line, which concludes that world opinion should go smartly into reverse and start cossetting South Africa rather than excluding it, overlooks two facts. First, De Klerk acted out of instincts not of generosity but survival. The only alternative to a deal with the blacks would be a siege economy defended by military might. Frank Chikane, general secretary of the South African Council of Churches, puts this as the very reason for his optimism. He told me: "The whites and the business community are pushing De Klerk's line because they think it will secure their own future."

But second, consider the ominous anecdotal detail that there are parts of Soweto, the black city outside Johannesburg, where the president is already known as Comrade De Klerk. This attests to the popularity he's already achieved in some black quarters because he is seen as the prime mover and shaker of an insupportable status quo. But it also speaks for the scathing hostility with which Mandela, De Klerk's selected partner in the deal, is sometimes regarded. "Comrade" is a bitter joke. It says that De Klerk has put one over the real comrades, is in charge of the agenda, has absorbed them into his plan. It gives a taste of the many-faceted political problem the ANC faces, as it decides, over the coming months, what of the past to insistently remember and what to pragmatically forget.

Some things no black leader can ever abandon. One is the commitment to a non-racial Parliament. In the pre-talks fencing about the protection of minority rights, most attention focused on the upper House, to dilute the black power of universal suffrage in the lower. De Klerk hinted at "cultural" (i.e. ethnic) vetoes in the second chamber, not only for the whites but for Coloureds and Indians as well. Somewhere here is supposed to lie a solution to the conundrum of how power can be shared between minorities and a majority.

No black save one I met could imagine such a blatant preserving of the racial political base. Chikane told me that one of his party pieces was to tell British and American officials, who would love to find a middle way, that if they can think of a system that is not based on one-person, one-vote, but is nonetheless democratic and non-racial, he will be happy to consider it. So far they have not met the challenge. To Chikane, they are pursuing a chimera, and Cyril Ramaphosa, the black trade union leader and a major contender in due time to succeed Mandela in the ANC, is equally adamant. "Ethnic grouping can never be compromised", he told me.

Many whites, I'm sure, are so steeped in racial thinking that they don't understand the profundity of this point. Nor are they alone. The Rev Jerry Mosala, president of Azapo, the Black Consciousness movement which opposes the talks, doesn't believe the ANC are serious. They can't possibly compromise, I suggested to him. "I think they will", he replied, adamantine certitude reinforced by donnish manner.

Other ways round will have to be found, but they will tax the collective ingenuity. The government side has done a lot of work on some kind of federal structure, again to water down black power. "It seems to me a viable option", said Roelf Meyer, the deputy minister for constitutional development. Another ploy relates to the powers of the second chamber; in Namibia, by creating something almost as impotent as the House of Lords, the constitution-makers persuaded the liberation leader, Sam Nujoma, to reverse his attitude towards the second chamber. More drastic options for pacifying white fears could even involve a period of transitional government, evolving from white to black over a fixed period. But all this is virgin ground. The only fixed point in it is the ANC's refusal, for its political survival if no other reason, to countenance any trace of an ethnic vote.

Other matters, by contrast, will require more from them. Here we get closer to understanding how many words they will have to eat: and why, therefore, it is their sensibilities, at the head of a less disciplined multitude than De Klerk represents, which need most careful appreciation.

Their first defeat will be over who sits at the table. There's no way a settlement can be reached without the participation of Chief Gatsha Buthelezi, the Zulu homeland leader and head of Inkatha, with close links to the Government and a less militant stance against some government attitudes — for example about "simplistic" majority rule. Other homeland leaders, to ministers' chagrin, have come swiftly into line behind the ANC, but Buthelezi is a quite different case. The table may need to be round, thus obviating the need to determine which side he is on. But John Kane-Berman, head of the Institute of Race Relations, may not be exaggerating when he says: "Any attempt to exclude Buthelezi and Inkatha from a constitutional deal will see civil war in South Africa."

The second, more demanding sacrifice the ANC will have to make concerns their economic attitudes. Here more than anywhere the years of their political ostracism are apparent. Among the black leaders I spoke to, economic opinion ranged from elementary ignorance to vulgar Marxism with little in between.

Seen from somewhere like the KTC squatter camp

outside Cape Town, an economic theory based entirely on the need for redistribution of wealth acquires irresistible force. Here thousands of migrants, mostly from the Ciskei, live in primitive shacks without water, heat or light. After a night storm, the children are too wet to come to school because the roofs have leaked. The best school-rooms consist of discarded ships' containers, winched into place out of the puny welfare funds of foreign governments, Britain's included. The teachers are not paid, except from money turned capriciously on and off by foreign companies. The unfailing stoic dignity of those who live here — somehow clean, somehow clothed, somehow civil — cannot diminish their status as victims of more economic injustice and incompetence than is to be seen anywhere else in the world. If the "new South Africa" does not give them some redress, it will hardly be worth bringing to birth.

The idea, furthermore, that big business has nothing to do with such manifestations of apartheid, because capitalism is "colour-blind" — an argument much beloved of Anglo-American and the other major organs of economic life now seeking to adapt themselves to a new order — is an extravagant insult to the intelligence. For many decades, capitalism and apartheid were intertwined: and to this day, capital has done nothing like what it could have done to mitigate the grossest inequalities.

What a new government could quickly do is, all the same, limited. In a country with not a single black aircraft pilot or train driver, more than anti-racist rhetoric will be needed to keep the economy moving. What the residents of KTC and a thousand other camps and misbegotten townships need, above all, is foreign imvestment on a massive scale in an economy which, for many years, foreigners have found repellent. According to Professor Terreblanche, to achieve 5.5 per cent growth for 10 years, a modest target given the horrific inheritance, South Africa will need $10 billion a year: a forbidding turn-round from the present net *outflow* of funds.

While plainly De Klerk and the whites will have to accept some of the "socialistic" redistribution they abominate, blacks face the tougher task of accepting that full socialism will not coexist with high investment. Eastern Europe is not its only graveyard, so is Africa itself where, in country after country, market economics are struggling for rebirth after experiments that failed.

Some black leaders glimpse the truth of this. "When I go to Tanzania and see people still living in shacks, I know we've got problems", Frank Chikane said. "Terror" Lekota, publicity secretary of the United Democratic Front, conceded that life would be more difficult if a new government alienated the capitalists. "We are banking on the business sector as part and parcel of the assets of this country" he said.

To get anywhere near fulfilling this, the ANC needs economic education but also political confidence. The greatest single fear must be that investment, which is now deterred by sanctions, will in future be deterred by black majority rule: a no-win scenario with a vengeance. To assist them towards a political deal that might minimise that prospect, the ANC needs every sign that the world understands their problems: which means that there should be no question of remitting sanctions yet. Maybe when a deal is done, and needs to be sold to the whites, the time would be right for a rugby tour, or even for granting South African Airways landing rights in New York. Meanwhile, pressure should be kept up now, to give credibility to what still looks fantastic: a party that has not had to think for 40 years making common cause with one that was banned from doing so.

Both parties want the process to move at speed. Both are well aware of the danger each faces from losing momentum. But there are problems, especially on the black side. The ANC still needs a mandate to deal, and other black groupings need to settle their place. Serious talks are unlikely until the ANC's first conference, in December. A constituent assembly is looking more and more like the indispensable transitional vehicle. Although a deal could be ratified before September 1994 — the deadline set by the next all-white election — more time may elapse before President Mandela and Prime Minister De Klerk are installed at the head of a democratic government: years of blight the economy cannot afford.

As for the outcome, prophecies of joy and of doom have about equal currency. The optimists look to talks so cordial that the other players are soon forced to the table: Andries Treurnicht's Conservative Party wanting a slice of the action as much as Azapo and the Pan-Africanist Congress, now waiting for Mandela to fall on his face. Black and coloured influx into white areas and jobs will meanwhile proceed apace; schools will start to de-segregate; the stoic peons in KTC, like the violently politicised young blacks in Soweto and Natal, will see a better future looming; and the whites, ceasing to fear for their existence, will begin to act out Beyers Naude's dream that they should start asking blacks, "How do we become part of an African country?"

Maybe it is because the alternative picture is so frightful that such a rosy prophecy can, three months after Nelson Mandela's release, still be heard surprisingly often. For the other possibility is indeed terrible: a breakdown in discourse, the exchange of Treurnicht for De Klerk, the swamping of Mandela by the gangs of ultras whom only he can rise above, the emigration of the English, a civil war on many fronts, the armed might of Afrikaner power ranged for one last destructive battle against the unanswerable numerical superiority of those whose land they have plundered. The result would answer to De Klerk's most reiterated nightmare. Suicide.

3 Issues of the day

Alan Rusbridger

HOUSE of Delegates Debate on the Additional Appropriation Bill. Mr Kamal Panday *(Reservoir Hills)* rises to speak. "I just want to mention that on 2 February I came here for the opening of Parliament and while walking through the corridors I came across a number of wives of the hon members of the majority party," he begins. "One of them came over to me and told me that they had just been discussing me a little while before and that I was a hunk of a man. She said that I have a fantastic body and all of them had been saying that they wished they had a chance to date me. However, she said that apparently they had agreed in their discussion that it was so unfortunate that they were married."

There is an interjection. Mr Panday resumes.

"What they are doing now, I am able to come to the conclusion, is due to the fact that their wives are giving them a torrid time because of the comparison between them and I."

More interjections. The Chairman of the Ministers' Council rises to express concern: "Mr Chairman, this is the kind of rubbish that hits the newspapers and we cannot afford it."

The Chairman was right. Here it is. Alas, there is more rubbish to come this particular afternoon. The Deputy Minister attacks Mr H M Neerahoo as "an ignoramus of the highest order" shortly before two other frontbench members indulge in a little diversionary squabble about the merits of their respective suits.

The Leader of the Opposition is anxious. "I want to appeal for us to have discipline. Let us not look like clowns in the eyes of the community." But two minutes later he is defending his own clothes: "I can account for every suit in my wardrobe (*interjections*). I know there are many people who cannot account for how suits landed up in their wardrobes."

The fashion theme continues throughout the afternoon. Mr Mahmoud Rajab says he doesn't know where the hon Deputy Minister got his suit. The Deputy Minister is happy to tell him, but before he can do so Mr Kisten Moodley demands Mr Rajab that should own up about the source of his own. Mr Rajab is wounded: "Let me tell him that I do not, like him, buy from some little backdoor operation in Port Shepstone."

The House of Delegates is the Indian House. There are 45 members, most of them from Natal, voted in by an electorate of 51,000. The Leader of the Opposition is near the mark when he speaks of clowns in the eyes of the community. It is time to move to the next debating chamber in the modern, not altogether tasteful, extension to the Houses of Parliament in Cape Town. Here in the House of Representatives —

ISSUES OF THE DAY

the Coloureds' House — we may find Mr Anthony Reeves *(Klipspruit West)* complaining about the quality of back-up staff to his fellow mixed-race colleagues. "These people are meant to be qualified on paper, but a paper qualification does not always mean that the person can do the work," he moans. "One of the senior personnel members in the Department of Local Government, Housing and Agriculture often walks around the passages blowing funny noises on his hands and asking aloud: 'Who is . . . there?'"

He proceeds to accuse a senior official of corruption over housing contracts. "Last year there was a big hullabaloo in this regard. Every hon member asked me why I punched the official. The fact is that I did not punch him. I did invite him for a hiding though."

The Chairman cries Order! and advises the hon member that he should not punch anyone. Mr Reeves replies: "If I had punched the man I would not have a problem today because he would be dead *(interjections).*"

Life in the House of Representatives is, notwithstanding Mr Reeves, much duller than with the Delegates, largely because only 11 of the 85 MPs are not members of the same party, and that main party — Labour — is reasonably disciplined. Indeed, in today's debate the official opposition — all four of them — announces it will not take part.

The way the tricameral system has been set up means that the Whites will always have the final say, but the Representatives have grasped that they have limited powers to embarrass the Government (as on beach apartheid) and thus to gain concessions or block legislation (as with the Group Areas Act). The problem the Labour Party has is that it does not actually represent many people. Nor has it managed to wriggle free of its racial basis or to forge links with the broad liberation movement. Its influence is therefore limited.

The white MPs — the House of Assembly — meet in the tasteful wing of the building, a dark-wood and green-baize scaled-down version of the Commons. Here, too, they are discussing the Appropriation Bill. The invective is sharper and, one senses, more deeply felt. Mr PJ Paulus, the Conservative Party MP for Carletonville, is scornful of a National Party MP who claimed that whites were guilty of assaults in the mines. "The hon member wants us to believe that he is very knowledgeable as far as mining is concerned. I maintain that the hon member for George has never been near a mine. If he has the courage to go underground one day, once he reaches the shaft, he will tell his pants: 'Keep still, your master is not afraid.'"

The star of the chamber — the CP's answer to Dennis Skinner — is JH 'Koos' van der Merwe, who keeps up a constant and entertaining stream of Afrikaans heckling. Displays of 'compassion' bring out a chant of 'white-hater.' Anyone advocating integration invites a shout of "You're an Azanian, man!" or — the lowest slur — "President Mandela!"

When he makes a proper speech, it is pent-up with the bitterness of a race betrayed. "In the new South Africa, the Afrikaner people will have to depend on the goodwill of black people. . The Afrikaners will have the status of underlings and they will be sharecroppers."

The Speaker informs Mr van der Merwe that he has six seconds left. He launches a final, frenzied

ISSUES OF THE DAY

assault. "Then I want to say in the remaining six seconds that hon members will see the day when the CP becomes the parliament of this country, that these political frauds in the NP will be kicked out . . . *(interjection)* and that we will be governing this country . . . *(interjection)* and that the members of the NP have become alot of traitors . . . *(cries of 'Sis!')*. The Speaker does not like the word "traitor." Mr van de Merwe refuses to withdraw the slur, and is thrown out of the chamber. At last, something that feels just like home.

4 Don't get lippy, missy

Angella Johnson

THE WHITE bus driver's eyes widened in astonishment as I boarded behind an elderly passenger and produced one rand (23p) for a five-minute journey into the centre of Pretoria. "You can't ride on here," he blustered. I asked why not? "We don't carry your kind. You must get off," he replied.

"I don't understand. Is this bus not going to the city centre?" I said, feigning ignorance of Pretoria's strict apartheid bylaw which prevents black and white people using the same buses.

He looked contemptuously at my fare on the till counter. "This bus is for white people only. I can't carry you." I held my ground. "Do I have to *put* you off?" he said through clenched teeth, climbing out of his booth in a threatening manner.

My heart started pounding. It was the first of many occasions during my visit to South Africa that I was to experience blatant and aggressive racial prejudice for attempting to cross the barriers which still divide this colour-coded country.

DON'T GET LIPPY, MISSY

"You can try," I said, wrapping my arms around a metal handrail. The small group of mainly elderly and female passengers travelling at mid-day in South Africa's administrative capital shifted in their seats. Most looked embarrassed. No one spoke or met my eye, except a little girl who whispered excitedly to her mother and giggled.

It was as if a time-warp had taken me back to the deep South in the US in the late 1950s. So this was how Rosa Park must have felt when she refused to give up her seat to a white woman on that bus in Montgomery, Alabama, a small act of defiance that precipitated the Civil Rights Movement.

Apparently unsure of how to deal with the situation, the driver reluctantly took my fare. It was a modest victory. Last year a group of black men were arrested and beaten up when they boarded a similar bus during a campaign of defiance.

But my feeling of triumph was short-lived. On reaching the depot, surveyed by a statue of Paul Kruger, the last president of the Transvaal republic, I was marched into the administrator's office. "You know it is illegal to use these buses. They are not for your people. The law does not allow it," said the fat, moustachioed Afrikaner sitting behind the desk, as if chiding a child. "If you do it again you will be arrested. Use your own buses."

About an hour later I found out how real his threat was when I boarded a double-decker bus packed with white office workers on their way to comfortable, segregated suburbs. The grey-haired driver refused to take my money, saying: "You should know that your kind are not allowed on here." He stormed off the bus in exasperation when I refused to leave, and within minutes the passengers had been transferred to another bus, leaving me as the sole occupant.

The police were called and I was prevented from getting off by a number of drivers who blocked the exit. One, his face twisted with hatred, threatened revenge: "I know your face and we'll get you." By this time a large, mainly white crowd had gathered to witness the spectacle of a black who had broken the rules.

"Welcome to South Africa," said the policeman after he had charged me with illegally boarding a bus. A group of white youths cheered as I was bundled into the back of a yellow police van. At the police station I explained that I was a tourist and was unaware that South Africa had these laws. Again the system appeared unable to cope and I was released a couple of hours later.

Buses were desegregated only a couple of months ago in Johannesburg, but Pretoria retains a law which maintains different vehicles for whites and nonwhites. Such petty apartheid continues to thrive in conservative areas where local councils grimly cling to the crumbling relics of more than 40 years of white supremacy.

"Pretoria is the home of apartheid," said Shadrack, a tall young black security guard who had begged me not to attempt my bus journey. "Some things have opened up, but there are still places where we are not welcome."

Most white South Africans agreed that Pretoria was the city where discrimination was still deeply embedded. Despite superficial changes, apartheid's fundamental social structures remain firmly intact. "When you walk down the street, you still ask yourself whether you can walk into any restaurant," said Sophia Masebo, a 27-year-old office worker who lives in Soweto with her parents, two sisters, and two brothers in three-room house.

It was surprisingly easy to lose sight of the various ways in which segregation is being unofficially maintained throughout the country. I soon accepted that some shop assistants would try to deal with white customers first, and that many restaurants would discreetly seat blacks in empty, dark corners so as not to spoil the ambience for their white clientele.

I LEARNED to spot the bars, restaurants, and cafes where blacks were not welcome: invariably they had a little notice over the door, saying: "Right of entrance reserved". "You can't sit there. All these tables are booked for a party at 2 pm," said the waitress as I and a friend entered the Krugersdorp branch of Mike's Kitchen, a national restaurant chain open to all races. The American-style, fast-food layout was only half full. Hurriedly we were ushered to a far corner. "This is a much better place anyway. You can have a private conversation."

I questioned whether in such a tiny town all the tables could be booked, and insisted on seating near the centre with the other customers. She turned to my white male companion and said apologetically: "Look, this is a CP (Conservative Party) town. If I put you with the other customers they will walk out. This is not personal, but I have to think about my business." Our premature departure was greeted by applause.

Krugersdorp, 13 km west of Johannesburg, is a small industrial town controlled by the CP. The poor black population from the nearby township of Munsieville shuffle along the drab streets, their the heads bowed. "There is an unofficial curfew for blacks here at nights," said Anne, a white widow who runs a corner store. "The CP wants to stop any integration. They are ruining my business because fewer black people seem to come into town these days, and they make sure they are out before dark."

By the time I entered the estate agent's office, my outrage had dulled. "I'm afraid I have nothing available for rent or sale," said the little old lady. "Why don't you try the Prudential?" I pointed to numerous property notices plastered on the wall and asked if they were unavailable because I was black. Her sun-wrinkled face took on a dull pinkish hue. "Not at all. If we had anything, you could probably live there, but you would have to get someone else to sign the papers."

That is how many wealthy Asians, Coloureds, and blacks manage to live semi-illegally in whites-only suburbs. One Johannesburg agent offered to arrange for a white signatory if I was prepared to pay extra, but warned that the property would have to be in one of the few already mixed "grey" areas. In trendy suburbs, like Hillbrow in Johannesburg, the colour bar has broken down over the years as whites moved out. Often the properties are overcrowded and badly maintained, but non-white tenants must pay extra for the privilege of living outside their settlements.

None of the subtle prejudices widespread in British society had prepared me for such insidiously entrenched racism. Even in liberal Johannesburg the sight of a black woman walking beside a white man is enough to make heads turn.

There is no denying that South Africa has become

a relatively freer country for many black people, at least in the cities. A black taxi driver told me: "This is paradise compared to what it was when we had to carry passes, and could only visit white areas to do domestic work." He pays nearly twice as much as the average white person for a studio flat in Hillbrow.

In Boksburg, a town notorious for banning black people from its lake and tennis courts, a silence fell over the bar of the Masonic Hotel as I entered. "Your kind are not allowed in here," said an outraged man big enough to play second row for the Springboks rugby team. When I retorted that I was a tourist, he got down from his stool and, towering over me, pointed his finger in my face: "Don't get lippy with me, missy. We don't take kindly to kaffirs who answer back." Tension rippled silently through the bar.

I waved my finger in his face, and demanded to see the manager. "You better not fuck with him . . . he don't like kaffirs any more than I do," he sneered. Eventually a portly pool player suggested, not unkindly, that I have my afternoon drink somewhere else.

When I related the incident to Beyers de Klerk, former mayor of Boksburg and leader of the local Conservative party, he described the hotel as "one of the white man's last drinking holes. The Supreme Court stopped us keeping blacks out of our lake and it's now being used by no one. Only three buildings in the town are now purely for white."

De Klerk, 48, believes in purity of the races. "When you mix black and white blood you get nothing: just a brown no one, a Coloured with no culture and usually intellectually inferior. That's why I believe separatism is the only way forward." He produced a well-thumbed Bible and read several passages from Deuteronomy and Matthew which, he said, bore out his claim that black people were inferior.

"I was a liberal until I began to study the scriptures and discovered that total segregation is holy in the eyes of the Lord. I'm not against the blacks, but they have a different set of standards. They are promiscuous, illiterate, and dirty. Democracy is not something they understand and, when this country gets black majority rule as it is bound to within the next couple of years, we will lose our capitalist way of life."

A bearded, florid-faced, potbellied millionaire property developer, De Klerk is proud of his Scottish, Irish, and Flemish ancestry. "God basically made black and white people. Everyone else has bastardised through interbreeding. Even if my life depended on a blood transfusion from someone of a different race, I'd refuse it."

It would be easy to dismiss this as the rambling of a mad man, but Beyers de Klerk claims to be representative of the 40 per cent of white South Africans who support the two right-wing parties, the CP and the para-military Afrikaner Weerstandsbeweging. The CP — claiming to be the old National Party of the 1940s — believes in partition into industrialised, whites-only states linked to economically subservient black areas.

"Six months after this country gets a black president, I predict a white revolution which will be one hell of a bloodbath": De Klerk produced a handgun which, he said, he always carried.

At Utopia, a beautiful resort tucked between mountains at the end of a dirt road, Herman, the black gate attendant, refused to hand over the keys to my chalet. "Have you made special arrangements?" So off we went to see the manager who had accepted my booking the previous morning. "You should have asked if we were multiracial," she retorted when I insisted that she honour my booking. "This is a private place . . . not even Indians are allowed in.

Utopia, a popular get-away-from-it-all for white urban families, used to have a sign at its front gate which read, "No dogs, no blacks, no motorcycles". Herman said the words "no blacks" were erased earlier this year but, while they now allowed dogs, black people were accepted only as as domestic workers.

Most people accept that this kind of South Africa is dying and that black people are in the ascendant, and I came away optimistic that the tide of change is unstoppable. Large numbers of whites recognise that improvements for the blacks are the only way to maintain the country's first-world status.

Conditions were marginally better than I expected: in the cities especially, apartheid's demarcation lines have become less clearly defined. The different races can now use the same toilets, get married, and eat in the same places — even if it means sitting on opposite sides of a room — but they are still segregated by housing, education, and health care. It was difficult to accept that people of different colours continue to be prohibited from living in the same area. Some have circumvented the law, but only through the goodwill of white liberals.

That there is a growing Asian, Coloured, and black middle class is undeniable. Some of the homes in affluent Diepkloof Extension, in Soweto would not look out of place in London suburbs such as Hampstead and Highgate. But I found distressing levels of depression and deprivation among the majority of blacks. It is difficult to describe the choking stench from the sewage in the streets of the cramped squatter camps that fringe many black townships.

So the country may be in a state of transition, but apartheid is alive and kicking and it will take time to push racism underground.

On my return, two English women were complaining about the toilet at Heathrow. "It's like bleeding Bombay in there," said one. "You go in an' 'ave a look. A bloody little India." I went to see for myself. Two Asian cleaning women, engrossed in conversation, were standing in a corner with their buckets and mops. The place was pristine.

5 One for the road

Roger Omond

THE WORKING class Afrikaner with the letters spelling out "LOVE" on the knuckles of his left hand paraphrased Shakespeare. "If it were done when 'tis done, then 'twere well it was done quickly." He took another sip of his Castle lager and put it more simply. "We've got to trust De Klerk. He's our leader. He knows what has to be done. And we know that we've got to change soon. Even though some people may think it's too fast."

This was not an educated, smooth and sophisticated Afrikaner yuppie with a BMW and a Volkswagen for the wife who can be found in any one of the new middle-class suburbs dotted around South Africa. This was a man who works in a stone-crushing firm in the town of Ficksburg which has a white population of 4,800 and 30,000 blacks. It is in the heart of what all South Aricans call the "platteland." Literally it means flatlands. Mythology has it that the platteland is inhabited almost exclusively by Afrikaner flat earthers. His attitude to the momentous changes now taking place in the country, perhaps surprisingly, was not untypical. Seated next to him in one of three bars in the one-star New Ficksburg Hotel — the only hotel in town — was a Free State farmer. This is the breed of white who is supposed to pay his labourers the worst, exploit them the most and vote for the most right-wing politician available. This one, however, was perhaps not so typical. For one, he wore gold earrings. For another, he had his thinning blonde hair plaited and then wound up on top of his head. It was an intricate arrangement and he was rather an exotic sight amid all the Rotarians, Lions, and Round Tablers who were in the pub for an hour's serious drinking before an induction dinner.

The ear-ringed farmer also supported Mr De Klerk. "We all know that we've got to change," he said. "We just couldn't go on as we were. The whole bloody world was against us. And besides. I've got nothing against the blacks. I need them. But they also need me."

This was a constant refrain throughout the Free State — the interdependence of the races. Sometimes it hid, not very successfully, a master-servant relationship based on race that the white person speaking would not like disturbed. Much of it is paternalistic. But these are perhaps early days in the shake-up that the psyche of the Afrikaner is going through.

The farmer went on: "Of course there are people — in the Conservative Party and the Afrikaner Weerstandsbeweging (AWB) — who can't take all this change. But me? I know that I can't support the CP. For one thing all my labourers will just get up and go, and then where will I be?"

Another Ficksburg resident confirmed, not surprisingly, that right-wing whites were unpopular with local blacks. "One of our local shop owners went into politics for the CP," he said. "His business dropped by 90 per cent in a couple of days." Gone are the days, virtually everybody I spoke to said, when the Afrikaners could tell the world, or even its own blacks, to go to hell.

Ficksburg, which serves mainly as a warehousing centre for Lesotho, the small landlocked client state just over the river, knows this better than most. It suffered for Pretoria's policies when President P W Botha closed the border to Lesotho. As 2.2 million people cross through every year — second only in number to Jan Smut's airport's entry rate — Ficksburg came to an almost total standstill when the squeeze, ultimately successful from Mr Botha's point of view, was put on Lesotho.

This is, as Alan Paton might have said, a beautiful land. It would be instantly familiar to anybody who has ever seen a western movie. The flat sparseness of the central Free State around the capital, Bloemfontein, gradually gives way to greener, hillier, wheatlands with the occasional rocky outcrop. It could be used, in post-apartheid South Africa, as the territory to make boerewors (the Afrikaner speciality — spicy beef sausages) westerns.

On the other hand, nobody would say that the land around Bloemfontein is beautiful, except those who own it. There is a fierce attachment to the land that goes deep into the heart and soul of Afrikanerdom. Time and again people came up with the refrain: "FW must beware that he doesn't make us think that he wants to give away the land." It does not need spelling out that the fear is the land will be given to the blacks. Bloemfontein itself used to be regarded as one of the sleepier hollows of South Africa. It was made the judicial capital of the country when the union was formed in 1910. The northern states of the Transvaal and Free State made sure that they got most of the perks of unification. Pretoria was made the administrative capital. The Cape got the parliamentary capital. English-speaking Natal got nothing: its representatives at the National Convention are reputed to have played bridge at night while the Afrikaners plotted and schemed.

They still take their politics more seriously than English-speaking South Africans; not unnaturally as they have been ruling the country, in one form or another, since 1910. They pay a price for this single-mindedness, however. A Bloemfontein psychologist said that the Afrikaners were much more rigid, less open to new ideas, and less able to respond to therapy when they needed it. The same psychologist, as we sat in one of the new high-rise office blocks that have transformed Bloemfontein into a mixture of Victorian and skyscraper architecture, added to this point. "Now that De Klerk is changing us so much, what happens to those loyal members of the state who have no role? What about all those security policemen who felt, and were told, that they were doing such an important job in keeping white civilisation safe from godless communism? They're wandering around without direction. They're angry and bewildered."

This is a question that worries many South Africans, English or Afrikaans-speaking. It is from the ranks of those people that the leader of the neo-Nazi AWB, Eugene TerreBlanche, claims he gets most support. Their potential for causing trouble is enormous.

ONE FOR THE ROAD

The Bloemfontein psychologist gave a little reassurance. "They need direction. They've little initiative on their own because they've been so used to following orders. But if they find another direction . . ."

South Africa almost by definition is not a consensus society. But in talks around the Free State there was broad agreement that the far right had had its day and that there was almost a ritualistic pattern in their protests against Mr De Klerk's reforms. It was almost as if they were going through the motions not really believing that they would win the day.

In Ficksburg, sitting in his comfortable office overlooking the central square, a businessman pointed to another error that the far right had made. "Now they're talking about staying away from work, about crippling the railways and airways and government offices for two or three days in protest. But I tell you, man, that we've seen this type of thing before, and it's always been the blacks and the left-wingers that have gone into boycotts and all those things. It just doesn't feel right for good Afrikaners — even if they're misguided — to do those things."

The far right's views are well-known, the views of ordinary Afrikaners less so. "You want to know what middle class people in Bloemfontein feel?" asked the psychologist. "I'll tell you. They don't talk about it. They just ignore it."

Some do not. In a luxurious house close to the official Bloemfontein residence of the State President, a woman in her early seventies spoke of her hopes and fears. "I'm broadly on the government's side," she said. But I do fear the CP and the AWB. I think if black children come toyi-toying down the street into the white suburbs, there'll be trouble. Maybe nobody will shoot, but there will be violence." Her husband, a prosperous surgeon who weighs words and talks with deliberation — sometimes to the irritation of his wife — pointed to another common worry. "Whites are concerned about their economic future as well. We're worried now, if it comes to that. We have a mortgage rate of 20 per cent and inflation at 15 per cent. We fear corruption. We don't want a corrupt government."

No irony was, apparently, intended but one of the main accusations levelled against the P W Botha presidency was the extent of white corruption. It had started under his predecessor, B J Vorster, when the Department of Information, controlled by that rigid and upright conservative, Connie Mulder, concluded that it was permissible to bribe or blackmail support from foreign governments and journalists.

From there it was a short step to doing the same thing inside the country and soon hundreds of thousands of rands were being scooped up for private consumption, and it has continued in many different government departments controlled by God-fearing Afrikaners. So the prospect of a corrupt black government sometime in the future is a little ironic. But white South Africa has been brought up on tales of black corruption and inefficiency. Even this urbane and intelligent Afrikaner is not exempt from his history.

"The blacks want more money. The whites will have to share. I don't know what AngloAmerican thinks, but I know that my shares won't be worth as much in a few years.

"The blacks will want something in between Russia and Britain, some welfare state. Where's the money to come from? There are too many people in this country already. There's too much poverty, I know; what we need is sanctions to be lifted and a new Marshall Plan."

This, too, was common to many Afrikaners: sanctions must go. On the one hand, they said that sanctions had hurt. On the other they all refused to say that sanctions had forced a change in policy. All but one — the Ficksburg businessman, well built, in his early forties, said that the sports boycott had hurt.

"But it affected only people of my generation," he said. "We were sports mad. Then the boycott started. I was against it. Then I started thinking: why were we refusing to play against Maoris, refusing to let Basil D'Oliviera into the country? And my views began to change. We then had a bit of multi-racial sport, then a lot more.

"But still the boycott wasn't lifted and we started getting angry about it. And you know what? None of my kids are crazy about sport now, they've never seen a Springbok team playing properly against an international team."

The Bloemfontein surgeon's son pointed to an important aspect that the African National Congress now is beginning to address seriously: the fear of whites, particularly Afrikaners, that they will lose their culture when — and most accept that it is inevitable — a black government takes over. "I don't mind living next door to blacks if they've got the money to stay in white suburbs. But I don't want paupers here. And just as I respect their culture, they must respect mine. My language, my standards."

Over another Castle lager, the Ficksburg stone-crusher also spoke of standards. "I've got a nine-year-old daughter," he said. "I get worried about her schooling if they let blacks in. What'll happen to her then? What kind of job will she be able to get?"

Standards and what the neighbours think are factors in much of Afrikaner politics. It is part of the rigidity that the Bloemfontein psychologist mentioned; that and the fact that for all the years of National Party Government there has been tremendous pressure to conform and not to leave the laager. Those who have left have suffered: the most extreme examples being people like Bram Fisher, Beyers Naude, and even Frederick Van Zyl Slabbert.

But this pressure to conform, says an Afrikaner like the writer Andre Brink, is an abberation in Afrikaner history. The volk in days gone by were rugged individualists who trekked to pastures new if their neighbours intruded. There was a time, from the 1950s until the late 1960s when, mainly under Dr Hendrik Verwoerd, conformity was the norm; when questioning the volksleier (people's leader) was somewhere between treason and blasphemy. As Afrikaners became more self-confident, fissures grew again.

"The first time that we had a black to stay overnight," said another Ficksburg resident, "I did think what the neighbours would say. Then I thought what the hell, I've got to put up with their barking dog."

Just why there has been this increasing friendliness between black and white, even to the extent of a black sleeping in a white house on the platteland, is one of the great unanswered questions. The mother of a young man who served in the South African Defence Force in Angola gave one view.

"Our boy was in a truck that broke down. He got stuck on the side of the road for 10 days, with only his rations that should have been for a week. One of the blacks who trained with him passed in another truck. 'Hey man, you're not going to last until the army gets you out of here,' the black told him. 'Take some of my rations.'

"But our son refused. He knew that the black chap was off to the front and soon would be fighting for South Africa. He didn't want to take his food. Then a few hours later he found that the black had left half his rations anyway.

"That made a tremendous impression. And I think a lot of our children who got to know blacks in situations like that began to have new thoughts."

The militaristic state so beloved of P W Botha and the present — but possibly soon to retire Minister of Defence Magnus Malan — was highly unpopular with all the young Afrikaners I spoke to. Their two years' service, they thought, was a waste of time. One or two had become embittered by fighting a war for reasons never made clear.

A hitchhiker, moustachioed, in his mid-twenties, spoke enviously of his brother. "He's only got to do a year in the army now," he said. This man, an encyclopaedia salesmen on his way to the small village of Westminster, also thought that Mr De Klerk had to be trusted. "It's mainly the older people who are against it," he said. "You can't blame them really. They've grown up in one way and can't adjust like us young people."

This part of the Free State, although Afrikaners may regard it as their own, shows some foreign influence in the names of towns: apart from Westminster, there are villages called Marseilles, Hobhouse (named after the suffragette and opponent of the British war against the Boers at the turn of the century) and Shannon. Emily Hobhouse is still remembered — indeed a South African submarine was named after her — more for her support for the Boers than for her later warnings that the racial policy of those Boer War generals like Smuts and Botha and Hertzog would bring international opprobrium down on the heads of their descendants.

Many of the sons and daughters of Afrikanerdom now hope, in the words of one Ficksburg resident, that "the world will take note of how we're changing from within, renewing ourselves, and taking a giant step towards a free society."

6 Brothers in lore

David Beresford

THE UNEASINESS of fraternal ties is a commonplace. "Between brothers, two witnesses and a notary," as the Spanish proverb has it, echoing Hesiod in the 8th century BC: "When you deal with your brother, be pleasant, but get a witness." And there is a certain unease about one of the most remarkable fraternal ties in contemporary politics: that between "FW" and "Wimpie " — South Africa's new State President, Frederick de Klerk, and one of the most outstanding Afrikaner intellectuals, Willem. To some extent the unease — and one hastens to say it goes no further than that, because they seem to be good friends — might be attributed to a reversal of roles.

Wimpie, after all, was big brother. Not only is he eight years the senior, but he was the trail blazer — along whose brilliant path his kid brother has belatedly trod, with now sensational effect. It was Wimpie who introduced that most familiar of words to the South African political lexicon: *verligte,* or enlightened. And now it is FW who is giving new force to the word with a dazzling display of enlightenment from an office which, to say the least, is unaccustomed to it. That both men should have had a considerable impact on South African politics is hardly surprising, given their backgrounds. That they should have done so in the way in which they have is a little more difficult to puzzle out.

Active involvement in politics has been a long-running tradition in the De Klerk family: a great-grandfather was a senator, a grandfather made three unsuccessful bids to become an MP (he was equally unsuccessful as a guerrilla, ending up as a PoW during the Boer War) and their father a cabinet minister. It was the career of the father, Jan de Klerk, that makes the present reputation of the sons a little surprising. He was a teacher, of Afrikaans and history, who rose through the National Party ranks to become Transvaal general secretary, a provincial councillor, a senator, Minister of the Interior (among other portfolios) and eventually President of the Senate, a post he held until his retirement in 1976. As a member of the cabinets of both J G Strijdom and Hendrik Verwoerd, De Klerk senior was necessarily a man of conservative hue.

He was responsible, for example, for the early implementation of the Mixed Marriages Act and Immorality Act — those two pieces of legislation so reminiscent of Nazism, prohibiting sex and marriage across the colour line — and agitated even against racial mixing in scientific organisations, against which there was no statutory bar. The relationship between the De Klerk family and the Strijdoms was a particularly important one. A sister of Senator De

The De Klerk brothers (Illustration: Peter Clarke)

Klerk married Strijdom himself — an extreme republican responsible for introducing many of the uglier aspects of apartheid during his four-year premiership. The senator and the prime minister were close friends, their families constantly visiting each other's homes and taking holidays together.

Despite this background, Wimpie insists that his father was himself a *verligte,* at least in the latter years of his life. One is tempted to dismiss this as a statement of filial loyalty in a time when *verligteheid* is fashionable, but it is probably true of the old man and it has a bearing on another interesting tradition in the De Klerk family — their religious allegiance. It is a little noted, but notable, fact about F W de Klerk that he is the first post-war Nationalist head of state who has not belonged to the predominant Dutch Reformed Church in South Africa, the *Nederduitse Gereformeerde Kerk* (NGK). Almost from its inception, in the mid-19th century, the De Klerk family has identified with the third and smallest of the DRC churches, the *Gereformeerde Kerk* (Reformed Church). Because in the early days they favoured short jackets against the more formal frock-coats of their co-religionists, they are popularly known as the *Doppers* — the word seemingly coming from the Cape Dutch word *doppen,* variously translated as to husk, to strip away the covering, or to judge.

Created out of the schism which followed the Great Trek — a formative event in the history of Afrikanerdom which, ironically, was disavowed by the NGK at the time — the *Gereformeerde Kerk* was, at least in its early days, the most strictly Calvinist. But though fundamentalist in character, its determinedly scriptural assessment of social policy has distanced it from party politics and made it the most open-minded and, ultimately, progressive of the DRC trio. They are what is known in Afrikaans as *konsekwent:* having made a moral judgment they are locked into the logic of it, wherever it might take them. And it is probably not fanciful to read into this tradition the apparent political flexibility of the De Klerks; the senator's conversion from the extremes of the Strijdom era to the verities of *verligteheid;* the emergence of Willem from such a conservative background and possibly — but only possibly, because this remains the central question in contemporary South African politics — the conversion of FW.

The *Gereformeerde Kerk* is centred at Potchefstroom, a small southern Transvaal town which was once the capital of the old South African Republic, but today can boast of little more than a sausage industry, the world's largest salt factory and a campus which labours under the name of the Potchefstroom University for Christian Higher Education. This is the university which Wimpie attended — followed later by his brother — and where he quickly won a reputation as an outstanding, if angry, young man. Chairman of the Potchefstroom Students Representative Council for three years and president of the student organisation *Afrikaanse Studentebond* one of his fondest memories of university days was of steering a resolution through the annual congress of the national body, calling for talks with black students at the liberal University of the Witwatersrand. For this he was promptly summoned to the home of the then Nationalist prime minister, D F Malan, for a personal dressing-down.

It was the first of many clashes which Wimpie was

to have with the political leadership of Afrikanerdom. He left university to become a Gereformeerde *dominee* (minister) but returned to academic life as professor of philosophy and psychology at "Potch" in 1966. He then began to carve out a reputation for himself as a commentator — initially as editor of the influential Potchefstroom journal closely associated with the Doppers, *Woord en Daad* (Word and Deed), in which he used to lacerate apartheid. His journalistic career prospered, but eventually foundered on differences with the political establishment. In 1973 he became editor of *Die Transvaaler* — the newspaper in which Verwoerd used to peddle his racist and vaguely anti-semitic views during the war years — but was ousted in what was seen at the time as an attempt to placate the more conservative Treurnicht wing of the National Party. He went on to take the editorship of the country's largest-circulating Afrikaans newspaper, *Rapport,* but was again too belligerently *verligte* for the party and was fired in 1987. Today he is back in academia, teaching communications at the Rand Afrikaans University in Johannesburg.

Despite Wimpie's many clashes with the establishment, his stormy career can be seen as something of a repudiation of popular — and, in particular, international — perceptions of Afrikanerdom, in that he has never actually been excluded from his community. He has been, for example, a contented member of the *Broederbond* since his mid-20s and for at least a decade has sat on the executive of what is generally presented as an ultra-conservative, even sinister, organisation. A career in parliamentary politics has always been his for the asking.

He has been offered a seat at least four times and

even P W Botha tried to persuade him to sit on the President's Council. More recently he was widely punted as the putative leader of the re-formed liberal opposition, the Democratic Party — a development which would have given rise to the most dramatic instance of *broedertwis* (a clash between brothers) in South African history. But it was really wishful thinking: Wimpie has never been cut out for party politics. A fervent disciple of Emmanuel Kant as a young man, he is in his own words "a relativist, not an absolutist"; a typical *dominee,* working to sow the seeds of morality — a vocation which sits uneasily with the mores of professional politicians, for whom Wimpie has a barely disguised contempt. Essentially Wimpie is the son of Jan the teacher, while FW is the son of Jan the party hack.

The eight-year age difference between the brothers straddled their father's two professions and FW's career was firmly grounded in his childhood experiences, tagging along to political meetings and on the hustings with the senator. Wimpie's early memories of FW are of a passionate conciliator, "always manoeuvring for peace", to the extent that he would even mediate in clashes between his rebellious big brother and their parents. He was also an organisational man in the making, eschewing the sports field — which is so often the proving ground for Afrikaner youth — in favour of debating societies and the like. He followed Wimpie's footsteps to Potchefstroom, but was content to serve rather than dominate; a member of the SRC, but not its chairman. Nevertheless he was, like his brother, an outstanding student and took his BA LLB cum laude in 1958.

Practising for a while as an attorney in Vereeniging, he was tempted at one stage to follow Wimpie into academia when he was offered the Chair of Administrative Law at Potchefstroom. But he was saved from the ivory towers by his election to parliament for Vereeniging in 1972. His subsequent rise in the National Party was swift, if quiet. He reached cabinet rank within six years, at the age of 42, and was to hold a wide range of portfolios: Posts and Telecommunications, Social Welfare and Pensions, Sport and Recreation, Mines and Environmental Planning, Energy Affairs, Internal Affairs and National Education.

FW has been a frustrating figure for political commentators, who have always had difficulty in affixing a label to him. He has been well described as "the ultimate Teflon politician" — the man to whom nothing sticks. There was one landmark in his political career into which much has been read: his energetic efforts to prevent the 1982 split led by the then Transvaal leader of the National Party, Andries Treurnicht. To this day Treurnicht's Conservative Party insists that FW was on the brink of following them. But they probably mistook conciliation for consensus. Certainly, when he succeeded Treurnicht as provincial leader he harried the Conservatives with a gusto which hardly suggests affinity, however latent.

On the racial question the only, tenuous, insight into what may be FW's views are to be found in remarks made by his wife, Marike, to the inmates of an old-age home a few years ago, a tape-recording of which was subsequently leaked to an English-language newspaper in Pretoria. Marike has insisted that the published quotations were "literally made up of half-sentences", giving rise to something of a conundrum as to what the second half of such as the following sentences might have been: "The definition of a Coloured person in the population register is someone who is not black and is not white and is also not an Indian, in other words a non-person. They are the left-overs. They are the people that were left after the nations were sorted out."

Marike and FW are seemingly soul-mates (family tradition has it that when they met at Potchefstroom University he returned from his first date with her to announce to a room-mate: "I met my wife tonight."). Soul-mates or not, it is perhaps unfair to brand F W with his wife's comments. But at the same time it is difficult to escape the fundamental racism inherent in FW's defence of the euphemistic concept of "group rights". And his reputation for conservatism is apparently shared among his National Party colleagues, as was dramatically illustrated in the February 1989 leadership election, when the comparatively young and inexperienced Finance Minister, Barend du Plessis, came from nowhere to within a hairsbreadth of taking the succession (69 votes to 61).

Nearly 50 per cent of the caucus seemingly believed F W was not the man to lead the "new South Africa". In that they may yet prove to be wrong. One might wish that Wimpie were today in his kid brother's position. Wimpie's passionate belief in the universal franchise, his faith that Afrikanerdom's survival into the future can best be secured by its recognition of itself as merely one of the country's many indigenous peoples — "the white tribe of Africa" — is the sane perspective. But, politics having little to do with sanity, FW is perhaps the better man to lead South Africa out of its insanity. If the international community can get its act together and maintain the pressure on Pretoria needed to lock it into the path of real negotiation, it is conceivable that the *Dopper* in FW will take over and lead him to his finest act of conciliation. Which would make of the De Klerks a particularly memorable tale of two brothers.

7 Lion in dove's clothing

David Beresford

THOMAS PAINE'S observation — that titles are nicknames and every nickname a title — is a maxim which comes to mind where Chief Mangosuthu Gatsha Buthelezi is concerned. Names and titles have always been somehow crucial to the man.

Marshall McLuhan once remarked that a man's name is "a numbing blow from which he never recovers". Which is a moot point where the Zulu people are concerned. Take, for example, that greatest of Zulu chiefs, Shaka. He was called after "iShaka", the name given to an intestinal beetle which, according to medicinal folklore among the Zulus, caused menstrual irregularities in women. It was cruelly bestowed upon Shaka because of a dispute over his birth. He was said to have been conceived illegitimately in a roadside dalliance between his mother, Nandi, and his father, Senzangakona, chief of the then small Nguni clan known as the amaZulu (the Heavenly People).

As Donald R Morris, one of the biographers of

Shaka, recounts it, the couple had seemingly indulged in the practice known as ukuHlobonga, a form of petting falling short of full sexual intercourse. When Nandi was found to be pregnant, Senzangakona denied it was possible, disparagingly suggesting that it was the work of an iShaka. Eventually he was forced to concede, and legitimised the child by taking Nandi as his third, little-loved wife. But the name stuck, and it is open to conjecture that the humiliation at his birth gave Shaka the sense of insecurity and inferiority which motivated his ruthless rise to power and the creation of the Zulu empire.

Whether this represents a failure to recover from a "numbing blow" depends on one's assessment of his achievements. Certainly, if the accounts of early European traders are to be believed, Shaka's rule ranks in infamy with some of the worst excesses of the Hitler era.

Chief Buthelezi, it should be said, does not believe those early traders whom he has described — with his customary crude hyperbole — as "depraved liars" who "scattered their sperm around kwaZulu as other men scattered footsteps". His sensitivity about his ancestor's reputation — Shaka was childless and the ancestry is therefore indirect, through a brother — is understandable; the parallels between the two men are striking and Buthelezi likes to emphasise them. "King Shaka built a mighty empire through statesmanship and wisdom," he once told a public meeting, "and I have built the mighty Inkatha movement through statesmanship and wisdom."

There also appears to be some similarity in how the two men got their names. A couple of years ago, in an article on Buthelezi and Inkatha, I made passing reference to the derivation of his Christian name, Mangosuthu. The story was given to me by one of the chief's closest aides who said the name translated as "the lie of the Usuthu (royal house)".

According to the aide, there had been some differences at the time between the royal household and the then chief of the Buthelezi tribe. The Zulu monarch, King Solomon, decided to heal the breach by dispatching his sister, Princess Constance Magogo, to marry the older Buthelezi (by another account, the princess was in love with another man, and the arranged marriage was a heart-breaking affair for her). Princess Magogo, so the story goes, fell pregnant by the then chief Buthelezi, returned to her family in the Zulu capital of Ulundi, and gave birth to the present Buthelezi. But the princess was ill, and when a royal messenger arrived at the Buthelezi kraal to announce the good news, the father cried out, "It is a lie of the royal house", in disbelief that either the princess or the child could have survived.

As is usual when articles at all critical of Buthelezi are published, his letter of denunciation duly arrived at the Guardian. In the course of a lengthy diatribe he described the story of how he gained his name as untrue, but unfortunately failed to provide an alternative explanation.

Subsequently I ran into Donald R Morris in Windhoek on assignment for a Texas newspaper. Morris — who has an engaging way of introducing himself as an ex-CIA agent — claims a 20-odd year friendship with Buthelezi and, when asked if he knew the story, said the chief himself had told it to him. He insisted, however, that the name translated as "all praise to the Usuthu" and had been uttered as a cry of joy. But, according to a Zulu linguist, that translation is incorrect, and so the "lie of the Usuthu" stands.

For years Buthelezi was addressed in public by his other name, Gatsha — it apparently means "branch" — until he banned its use on the grounds that it was his mother's endearment and he did not want it cheapened by common usage. Newspapers quickly complied. A Natal journal had once been reduced to referring to him as "Nkosi (Lord) Buthelezi"; and another paper's news editor was roughed up when he visited Ulundi to try to convey apologies for publishing an article about a white farmer who had named his dog after the chief.

Buthelezi's devotion to his mother provides another parallel with Shaka. History is again dependent on one of those sperm-splattering traders but, if Henry Fynn is to be believed, Shaka mourned his mother's death with appalling acts of atrocity. Fynn estimated that 7,000 Zulus were massacred; 10 handmaidens were buried alive beside the dead woman, with their arms and legs broken; and Shaka ordered that in the ensuing year any woman found pregnant was to be slaughtered with the father of the child, and no crops were to be planted or milk drunk.

Buthelezi's adoration of his mother also appears to have bordered on the obsessive. A recent hagiography quotes the chief as saying of her: "No son is more aware that God smiled upon his mother than I am. I was shaped by a mother so filled with beauty, nobleness, and love that the pain of her passing away is intermingled with a sense of fierce pride, and nursed by joy in her remembrance. She came out of the past to me and my people as one of God's shining lights, and one of His reminders that His goodness is a good-

LION IN DOVE'S CLOTHING

ness He spreads among us in a special concern for who we are . . . Knowing how I was shaped by one so great, her passing has turned me to deeper levels of dedication to serve my people. I will, perforce, be a lion in the things we value and a dove in the service of Zulu brotherly and sisterly love."

Quite apart from what it says about his relationship with his mother, the quotation encapsulates some of the often contradictory strands which make up Buthelezi: the passionate Christian and equally passionate Zulu chauvinist; the bellicose lion who would also be seen as the dove of peace. The author, Alan Paton, a great admirer of Buthelezi, remarked to me before his death in 1988 that the chief was "a lover of Christ, a lover of humanity, a lover of South Africa, a Zulu. Sometimes you would think the Zulu came first".

But one characteristic which troubled Paton was Buthelezi's immense pride; others might describe it as overweening self-esteem. Paton recounted an occasion when Buthelezi had walked out of a hotel with him in Durban and a burly black man had thrown himself on his knees in front of the chief in the middle of the street. "I wouldn't want anyone to fall on his knees to me," said Paton. "But he (Buthelezi) took it as a matter of course." Paton found this understandable in a man who is above all else an aristocrat.

Buthelezi's pride in his ancestry and position is germane to the apparent contradictions between the "lion" and the "dove". His defenders often argue that his intolerance of criticism stems not from personal conceit but sensitivity to his status as a symbol of his people: insult Buthelezi and you insult the Zulu nation. As is the case with Mrs Thatcher, the kwaZulu

Chief Buthelezi (Illustration: Peter Clarke)

chief minister appears at times to be confused about who is sovereign (the Zulu king is Goodwill Zwelithini).

The lion-dove paradox bears directly on the question of responsibility for the regional civil war which has been raging for years in Natal. A memorable libel action over this culminated last month in an Appeal Court victory for the chief. The alleged libel, originally published by the Spectator, said: "His (Buthelezi's) claim to represent the sole non-violent alternative to Marxist revolution is questionable to say the least, and his well-drilled impi regiments are among the most thuggish operators in South Africa." When the article was republished by the small South African news magazine, Frontline, the chief promptly sued on grounds that it accused him of being a purveyor of violence.

In a defence of justification and fair comment, Frontline pointed to the chief's public speeches. Some quotations were bellicose in the extreme, such as one from a 1980 speech in which Buthelezi said: "If the scrawny cockerels which crow on dunghills will not scatter when we stamp our feet, we will grab their scrawny necks with our rough hands and squeeze them a little bit, and make them gasp. And then we will see what will happen. Someone said that the best form of defence is to be the first to attack."

And there were repeated references by Buthelezi to the justification of taking "an eye for an eye" which, under cross-examination, he said amounted to self-defence, but which the trial judge described as "proportional retaliatory violence rather than the use of force within the bounds of self-defence recognised in criminal law". None the less both the trial judge and Chief Justice Corbett — who handed down the Appeal Court finding — found for Buthelezi. Corbett agreed with the chief's statements that "the Zulu nation is a people steeped in the military tradition," and its members "have warrior blood coursing through [their] veins". "Military allusions and metaphors would thus appeal to and be understood by such audiences, and should not be taken too literally," Corbett said.

The judgment has proved contentious. In the volatile atmosphere of Natal it is difficult to avoid extending the familiar rubric that it ill behoves the man who strikes a match and shouts "Fire" in a crowded cinema to protest afterwards that the audience should not have taken him too literally. Corbett, who has an outstanding reputation as Chief Justice, is regarded as something of a liberal, and one is tempted to find in his judgment — as in Paton's attitude towards Buthelezi — traces of a liberal admiration for the "noble savage"; but it is an admiration which can sometimes show little appreciation for the consequences of savagery.

Buthelezi has some justification in protesting that he too is a victim of savagery: not only in Natal, but also in the rhetoric used by his opponents. In his denunciations of the ANC and its allies, for example, Buthelezi employs to some effect a position paper on negotiations, apparently put out by the ANC-affiliated South African Congress of Trade Unions, which says it is "inconceivable that the democratic movement and the broader national liberation movement can reach accommodation with the puppets in Inkatha.

"The hand of truce offered by Gatsha is a weak hand, and a sign that the people have made massive inroads into Inkatha's power base. The time is right to deliver the death blow to this enemy of the people . . . the snake that is poisoning the people of South Africa needs to be hit on the head . . . Gatsha must be dealt a serious blow, and the workers must show him that his attempts to divide the workers will be met with revolutionary violence."

There were high hopes that Nelson Mandela might have the stature and determination to calm Natal. But his appeal to the protagonists to throw their weapons into the sea has been ignored; his attempt to meet Buthelezi seemingly vetoed by the ANC.

The Zulu leader's trump card has always been seen as an alliance with white South Africa. But today it is doubtful whether the government believes such a card exists. As President F W de Klerk and Nelson Mandela display a growing rapport, the betting is that, however inconceivable a few months ago, the key alliance will eventually be between the ANC and the National Party. With hindsight Buthelezi would have been better advised to have made peace with the ANC, even at the cost of his own self-esteem. But that is a price he was not prepared to pay. He is, after all, a descendant of kings, a man who has cast himself in the mould of Shaka. And it is in that respect that the name, Mangosuthu Gatsha Buthelezi, may well contain the attributes that undermine the chief of the Zulus.

8 The hidden war

Alan Rusbridger

A LITTLE context helps in trying to explore South Africa's hidden civil war. Try this: since 1987, 1,000 more people have been killed in Natal than in 20 years of troubles in Northern Ireland. Until General Aoun started to wreak his own brand of havoc in Beirut, not even Lebanon could match the spectacular killing rate of South Africa's most English province.

Drive half a mile east of Pietermaritzburg to the Mountain Rise cemetery and you'll find some of the victims. Not, of course, in the carefully tended white area, with its marble headstones and neat grass verges. Nor in the Coloured, Indian or Jewish sectors. South Africans are buried as they were housed. So make your way to the blacks' graveyard on the hillside and simply count the crude mounds of dull red clay.

Most of them have at their head a rough wooden cross on which the rudimentary details of the deceased are recorded in Dymo tape. BS Zondi, aged 18, died 25. 05. 90. Mouli Mtombele aged 13: At rest 18. 4. 1990. Jaba Ngubane. 4. 4. 90, aged 29. There is no clue as to how these people met their deaths, nor to the lives they led — except on the grave of one Comrade Lucky Dlamini, where there is a bunch of plastic flowers with a scrawled message: "Our blood shall not spill in vain. One Azania. One Nation."

The figures are unreliable, but in the Pietermaritzburg and Natal Midlands area alone this year some 400 have died. In the past three years the death toll from the conflict in Natal is more than 3,500. Thousands of homes have been destroyed and tens of thousands of people made homeless.

Your journey into the war zone will probably start in Pietermaritzburg, which could pass as an English county town in the age before the chain stores moved in. Drive out past the Victoria Club, the Croquet Club and the cricket ground and head for the gentle green hills south-west of town. Edendale Valley, when you first see it, seems not unworthy of the name. The valley is a huge lush amphitheatre around which are scattered pinprick clusters of housing.

But drive on through the township of Imbali and up the Edendale Road and you start noticing oddities. Many of the houses are roofless and scorched. Others have old mattresses stuffed in the broken windows. Shops are barred up and abandoned. And large tracts of countryside — houses, fields, sheds — are devoid of human or animal life.

Then in the distance you notice a convoy of army Hippos crawling in convoy up the side of a hill. A red Ford Sierra swoops past, the driver fingering a shotgun in his lap. And an unassuming redbrick church you approach by the roadside turns out to be a dormitory for 300 people who have fled their neighbourhoods and have nowhere else to sleep. In the middle of the nave you'll find Anastasia Mcahumu resting on the floor with her two children, aged 14 and 11. Her house was burned down and all her belongings looted, she says, by supporters of Inkatha, Chief Buthelezi's organisation which has its powerbase in Natal and kwaZulu.

Knitting on an old mattress near the altar is Albertina, a retired kitchen worker, who fled her home in Kazibuzo when, she says, Inkatha supporters burned down her house and stole her belongings. "They demanded to see our Inkatha membership cards, but we're UDF and didn't have one. They stole our TV, our wall watch, our bicycle and our generator and set fire to the house. They had guns and knives. I don't know where we'll go now. I would rather sleep outside here in the street rather than go back to my neighbourhood."

Here, then, in the nave of St Francis of Assisi Church, Edendale, are the first clues to the awful bloodshed that has poisoned this Eden. UDF versus Inkatha. All the evidence from the monitoring groups who have followed the grim trail from township to mortuary suggests that the power struggle between the two groups is the major reason — or excuse — for the ever-escalating violence. A breakdown of 200 incidents logged by the Pietermaritzburg Crisis Co-ordinating Committee up to April 3 claimed that 195 were attacks by Inkatha or the police on non-Inkatha supporters. Eighty-five people died in those attacks. A quarter of all the bodies arriving at the Pietermaritzburg mortuary are women.

But before writing off the entire war as plain

Inkatha versus UDF one needs a little more context and a look at some of the players involved. Since the early 80s there has been increased tension between the more rural-based traditionalists — loyal to Inkatha — and the younger, more progressive urban population which has little sympathy with Zulu nationalism and which views Chief Buthelezi with considerable cynicism.

The formation of the UDF gave the more progressive elements a rallying cause and sparked off a recruiting drive. Inkatha was outraged at the UDF's success in signing up entire areas (so successful that knowledgeable observers believe that today there is not one Inkatha township left in the Durban area) and the antagonism between the two organisations erupted into sustained violence in September 1987.

But fatally intermingled with the political rivalry appears also to be plain old fashioned gangsterism. The sprawling squatter settlements spawned by rapid urbanisation were soon carved up into manors by thugs and "warlords" who regularly extorted money by force or the threat of force. Inkatha found it convenient to move in and convert this mafia to its own political ends. Anyone attempting to switch to the UDF, or to recruit for the rival cause, was soon eliminated.

In the settlement of Malakazi, for instance, an unofficial mayor called "Thousand" established himself and started taking rent from the community. Thousand was duly recruited or coerced into supporting the aims of Inkatha by a warlord named Shozi. Another local gang — the Amasinyoras — began life as an apolitical bunch of looters. Eventually they focused their attentions solely on houses lived in by supporters of the ANC, the UDF or the associated trade union, Cosatu.

Or consider one of the most notorious warlords, David Ntombela, 65, who rules the Vulindlela area at the top of the Edendale Valley. Mr Ntombela has one life as a kwaZulu MP, a member of the Inkatha Central Committee and a willing source of newspaper interviews in which he denounces violence as senseless.

Numerous witnesses know another Ntombela — as a man who shot and killed his own brother; as a man who was involved in killing an Elandskop woman shopkeeper, Mrs Mandla Mkhize, and her son in 1987; as a man who has been involved in the deaths of at least eight other political opponents since then.

When not addressing political meetings with Chief Buthelezi (at one of which he announced that anyone who did not belong to Inkatha should be killed) he roams around his patch with ammunition belts slung across his chest surrounded by armed guards.

The fact that David Ntombela has never been convicted of a murder says a lot about the role and commitment of the police — in particular the Zulu Police (ZP) — and legal authorities. Ntombela has faced charges of murder — and was even found to be responsible for the murder of Mrs Mkhize by an inquest magistrate. Nothing happened once the matter was referred to the Attorney General.

Several impartial witnesses testifying before a commission of inquiry into the violence have given evidence that they have seen the ZP and South African Riot police aid and abet Inkatha impi attacks. Several local gangsters have been spotted wearing the uniform of *kits-konstabels* [special constables]. Two black South African policemen living in the area went to the extent of taking out civil injunctions against members of the ZP to prevent them from harassing local residents. Police protest that it is difficult to find witnesses and evidence to use against perpetrators of violence (not that that has unduly hamperered their investigations into the ANC or its armed wing, MK). But there is a desperate shortage of manpower: one police station in Plessislaer for 300,000 people.

Until 32 Battalion of the South African Defence Force (SADF) was deployed earlier this month, large areas of Natal were ruled by gangs and guns. There was no recognisable law and no recognisable politics. But, unlike Lebanon or Northern Ireland, this was a conflict that was largely ignored by the media. Natal law still has the charge of "faction fighting" on its books as a way of dispensing with what it sees as tribal in-fighting. The media appears to have viewed the conflict in a similar light. It was "black-on-black." It was self-contained. It was horrendously complicated. It required a certain fluency in Zulu. Besides, as one news editor sought to explain: "If I tried to cover all the violence in South Africa I'd have the entire newsroom out permanently in the townships."

So the forgotten war raged on out of sight and mind. Even allowing for the fact that its victims had no representation in Cape Town or Pretoria, there appeared to be little political will to deal with the problem. Why? There is no shortage of conspiracy theories, not all of them easily dismissed in a country whose modern history is based on a giant conspiracy.

The Rev John Aitchison, a Natal University academic who has published the most thorough studies of the conflict based upon the efforts of his own monitoring teams, believes that the government has quietly condoned the civil war. The violence, he argues, has been a relatively cheap and self-contained method of keeping the ANC occupied against a surrogate force (Inkatha), while also ensuring that Inkatha itself has been pre-occupied and compliant.

There are signs of hope. In recent weeks both the UDF and Inkatha appear to be having more success in disciplining their supporters. The SADF has succeeded in restoring a semblance of order to the region. Businessmen — their employees unable safely to travel to work — have started lobbying the government. And the government, firmly committed to negotiating some sort of peaceful settlement, would almost certainly like to de-escalate the confrontation. Much depends on whether Inkatha, with its 1.7 million members, can afford quietly to sit back and watch its powerbase eroded even further. A May Day rally in the most sparsely-populated rural area on the South Coast was attended by an impresssive 15,000 UDF Comrades. John Aitchison believes Inkatha to be in a "state of barely suppressed hysteria" at the speed at which its support is evaporating. Much, therefore, depends on the quixotic character of Chief Buthelezi, who is rapidly losing his privileged status as the white man's favourite black man. His reponse to the Commission of Inquiry into the violence was not a hopeful omen. It came from Messrs Friedman and Friedman, Attorneys, and was a threat to institute libel proceedings against the witnesses and the chairman. Meanwhile the graveyard at Mountain Rise continues to accumulate mounds of dull red clay.

9 On patrol

Judy Rumbold

TAKE A STROLL past the dog pound at Protea Police Headquarters in Soweto and Baskervillian mayhem erupts. Alsatians the size of small family saloons slaver and snarl; their name tags read Hitler, Rambo, Strike.

At the wheel of patrol car Delta 1, Sergeant Duranty cuts a marginally more benign figure. He's in a chatty, just-been-fed mood as he careers around the maze of dirt-track roads, groping about under the dashboard with both hands while the car swerves violently and hazards a 100mph bid for freedom. "Are there many townships in London?".

From a stash of tear gas cannisters, rubber bullets and redundant bullet-proof vests ("they ruin the line of your shirt") Duranty produces a 200,000 watt Nite Blaster lamp and hands it to his partner, Sgt Smit. "When you're patrolling a pitch-black area full of pitch black people, you need extra light."

Smit plays musclebound Dobermann to Duranty's Jack Russell in exquisitely bad Crimplene trousers and Brut 45 marinade. He waves the lamp out of the window and trains it on the road ahead, shining the interrogatory beam in the face of every black pedestrian he passes. Their bleached-out features register weary contempt. "It's so dark round here we have this joke", says Duranty, "they only serve Milky Bars in the cinemas in Soweto, otherwise they'd bite their own fingers off".

The radio spits out a clipped command, and the Protea flying squad weave through the dense fug of Soweto night-time to the scene of the first complaint. Each of the 35 townships has its characteristic criminal, says Duranty. "Eldorado Park, the Coloured area, is the worst. They're all goofy people; they curse your mother, your father, and they're always trying to stab you with bottles". In Lenasia, populated largely by Indians, housebreaking is a major problem. "They're not very friendly; especially when you're trying to arrest them".

The car pulls up outside Jabavu community centre in White City. A throng of inquisitive neighbours form a makeshift people's court. The story has a familiar plot; a man reels back late from a visit to a shebeen and goes looking for his wife in the house next door. He fails to find her there so he lays into the neighbour's TV set with an axe Women in dressing gowns gather around, relishing the entertainment and the blustery cop show melodrama of the arrest. Smit and Duranty warm to their audience, making much of battering down an unlocked door and threatening death by 9 mm Parabellum. No one is fazed by the sight of guns being waved around like ice lollies; life has become cheap in Soweto. "If we shoot somebody here, it's just one of those things", says Duranty.

"Shoot somebody in a white area, on the other hand, and all hell's let loose".

The offender is handcuffed and shoved towards the car. Sgt Smit holds a pistol to his neck and calls him a dirty kaffir. They drive him to Kliptown police station where he is ordered to the floor and told to shut the hell up. He hasn't spoken a word.

Earlier in the afternoon, at Protea HQ, a lugubrious Lieutenant Colonel Halgryn sits flanked by his Police Star for 12 years' faithful service and an ornamental frog collection. He starts talking like a Sainsbury's cashier. "Weekdays are quiet but it picks up on a Friday after four." People go to shebeens, get drunk, they become violent, he says. "Housebreaking, theft, rape, robbery, and GBH. Six murders over a weekend is relatively quiet."

Halgryn reckons he's learnt from US style policing; on the wall is a plaque inscribed with a Gordon Gekko-ish proverb: "The winner is always part of the answer, the loser is always part of the problem". He ushers in one of his teenage Afrikaner winners: "This one's a goer," he says, like a pimp showing off his best trick. Lance Corporal Louwrens — "I'm in it for the uniform, the car chases and the arrests" — smells of soap and school and looks ill-equipped to troubleshoot a city riddled with, as the wall plaque goes, problematical losers.

Marked patrol cars, emblazoned with the emergency telephone number, have made a big difference in public attitudes towards the police, he says. "Previously, when white vans attended complaints, there was always antagonism; crowds would gather. With the new patrol cars, there is respect; people say "Here come the *real* police". Alternatively, they say here come the Boer pigs. It's 11 o'clock, and Smit and Duranty are being stoned by a 1,000-strong mob. Someone is trying to burn down their own house in order to purge the place of *itokoloshi* (evil spirits). The neighbours clearly object to the SAP's attempts at a verbal hosedown. Duranty calls the riot squad and fingers a teargas canister "You can't walk around here without getting your throat cut, basically. You have to have eyes all over your head."

A spluttering radio message summons them to a car collision between a policeman and two other drivers. All parties are wild-eyed, drunk and volatile. Kliptown police station is slow in getting a patrol van to the scene so that blood tests can be taken, and Duranty blames the inefficiency of the black policemen. "We're very low on manpower", he says, "nine blacks and only five whites — there's just not enough of us".

Smit and Duranty speed off to investigate a report of a prowler in a back yard. Smit is clearly weary of such workaday complaints. He's anxious to get on with the interesting stuff — chasing BMWs and Corollas stolen from affluent Johannesburg suburbs and engaging them in high-speed shoot-outs "we aim for the tyres, then the legs".

Half an hour later, radio control confirms a positive Toyota high-tailing it in the direction of Kliptown. Smit makes triumphant siren noises through his nose and leans out of the window pointing a loudhailer at a terrified driver "Oi, turn your lights on!" It's Smit's last nod in the direction of sensitive people-management before the real action begins.

10 Behind the wire

Alan Rusbridger

COLONEL R was anxious to explain the position to a foreigner who might not appreciate the nuances of the situation. "It's nothing to do with politics or colour," he said carefully. "It's more to do with the position of the police."

He paused, and considered how best he might spell it out to a Britisher. "It's really the same as your guys in Notting Hill. Every policeman here who steps on a black man's toe gets a thrashing. Right now, no white man in a black country can do anything right."

The statistics bear out the thrust, at least, of Colonel R's thinking. It's got so bad that policemen are leaving the force at a rate of 11 a day. In the Johannesburg area alone, nearly 1,000 policemen quit last year, complaining about pay and conditions. The most visible result — to the Britisher — is that white Johannesburg has turned into one large, sprawling security compound guarded over by the likes of Colonel R.

The Colonel ("no names, please. Ex-Rhodesian Army") runs an outfit called First Force. He employs

70 men — a lot of them former policemen — to patrol the richer suburbs of Johannesburg. "We do everything. Burglaries, banks, raping, escaping. I guess it's a bit like any big city."

But of course Johannesburg is not quite like any big city and the residents of the richer suburbs appear to have acknowledged the fact by changing the topography of their neighbourhood landscapes.

"I remember even five years ago all over Johannesburg the houses had lawns that went all the way down to the road, with elegant driveways," says Ronnie Barnes. "I don't think such a house exists anywhere now. They've all got barriers 1.8 metres high around them."

Ronnie Barnes should know, since his company, Barnes Fencing, supplies a good proportion of the glistening razor wire that nowadays adorns most garden walls in white Johannesburg. The fences are at least 1.8 metres high since that is the specification demanded by the claims-bruised insurance companies. Ronnie Barnes is not complaining: he has a R10 million (£2.27 million) turnover.

Like the Colonel, Ronnie is keen to draw the distinction between political and economic. "In all my years in this business I've never known a political attack. It's crime. All of a sudden life has changed. People ring up and ask for razor wire because they think it's the latest technology. It's nonsense, of course. The burglars just throw a blanket over the wire."

The security engineers have been working on that. A glossy promo in the latest issue of SA Home Owner advertises some state-of-the-art fencing, available in gold or silver finish at R9.50 per metre —

Sharktooth spikes. "Even a mattress is penetrated by these mean spikes," boasts the inventor. "We also tested it with a telephone directory. It sliced through immediately."

Drive around Johannesburg and the manifestations are everywhere. The walls, the wire, the dogs, the electronic gates, the lights and the signs advertising the particular security company guarding the premises: "*Your best form of defence is Attack Security systems.*" Security is the top selling point in all estate agents' brochures. Gun shops have never done so well. Arms magazines advise on the best little baby to stop an intruder in his tracks.

Sandton Sentry Security patrols 70 or so square miles of northern Johannesburg and pledges (as in "We promise, not guarantee") a response within five minutes to a punch on the panic button from any of the 1,500 clients on their books. Their sentries — most of them ex-policemen attracted by the pay — drive around the area all day and all night. The R90-a-month service assures you of basic response. Pay R170 and you're into personal calls every few hours just to check all is okay. The guards drop off a calling card just to let you know they've been by.

"We carry handcuffs, and can arrest people and turn them over to the police," says Mr A Montana, the general manager. "We don't shoot for the sake of shooting. We're very careful about that." (One of the more celebrated security guards, Louis van Schoor, recently claimed to have shot dead 34 people in five years.)

Dogs? Try Ian Brooks at K-9 Security. "Domestic customers tend to go for Alsatians and German Shepherds. Myself? I prefer Rottweillers, but we can't get enough of them. They take too long to raise. It's not economic. There's a big shortage of Rottweillers."

"It's a sad fact, but times are good for us. It's all the unemployment, I'm afraid. Unemployment equals a higher theft rate, equals good business for us."

Just because it's paranoid doesn't mean that the Greater Johannesburg area — or, more correctly, "The Reef" — isn't one of the most violent areas of the world. Ten of South Africa's 32 daily murders occur on the Reef — twice the rate of New York. The lifting of the reporting restrictions and the political instability has led to a torrent of reports in the papers about the general level of violence. Political violence in the country as a whole has claimed between 574 and 966 victims so far this year. The same rate of killing will see 4,000 deaths in 1990, against 1,403 last year — and 1989 was the worst year so far.

This is almost entirely so-called black-on-black violence, and thus, to put it crudely, of little direct impact on the white community. But when a man was necklaced in the heart of Hillbrow, white Johannesburg sat up and took notice.

Hillbrow is one the few genuinely (if unofficially) "grey" areas of urban South Africa, and is but a rubber bullet bounce from some of Johannesburg's most manicured neighbourhoods. Anyone looking out of their windows in elegant Houghton or Parktown that day would have seen the acrid plume of black smoke rising from the three tyres placed around the body of an unidentified man in an open lot next to the bustling flea market.

Hundreds of local people saw the incident, yet the police managed to miss it altogether, and the Fire Brigade records are blank. The city councillor for the area promptly called for the army to be brought in on patrols since it was obvious that the police couldn't cope. Figures released the following day showed a 100 per cent rise in attacks on elderly whites. A Democratic Party MP claimed there were now six times as many private security guards as there were policemen in South Africa. The next thing was the panic over the story of a panic button that had failed. A Sandton woman was raped when the alarm to Super Cops failed to work. The next day, the figures for stolen cars were released: 72,000 in one year. South African cars now come with so many disabling devices that would-be thieves are often compelled to attack the driver in order to get at the portable hardware. The Mazda RXi now comes with a panic button which will set off the car alarm and unlock the doors if you're attacked while approaching it. Another button inside will scream and lock the doors if you're attacked while driving. A security columnist in one of the papers advised whites against giving their domestic the keys to the front doors. "Let's be honest," Mr Montana of Sandton Sentry Security told me, "a lot of it is inside jobs — maids and their boyfriends."

The enemy without, the enemy within. The week we were there the government announced handsome increases in police pay in a bid to stem the haemorrhage of staff. It may not be enough. One policeman explained: "I joined the police force to serve the community. But in some areas I am hated, spat on even. There is no respect for the honest working cop."

One more headache for FW, and for whoever succeeds him. Meanwhile Colonel R, a white man in a black country, will continue to do quite nicely, thank you.

11 Learning and losing

Douglas Morrison

THE FINAL FRUIT of apartheid education, says Ken Hartshorne, is a particularly bitter and disturbing variety — a generation of young black people who have forgotten how to learn. "What you've had is a complete breakdown in the learning process."

Dr Hartshorne, consultant to the Centre for Continuing Education at the University of the Witwatersrand and a long time critic of the existing system, is one of many involved in education who agree that the schooling of black South Africans has achieved an almost Orwellian perfection — producing people who do not know how to learn, who do not want to learn, and who are incapable of responding to the normal social processes by which learning takes place.

John Samuel, national director of the South African Committee for Higher Education, estimates that since 1985 up to 100,000 children a year have been affected in this way, and that it now shows up in what the state terms "anti-social behaviour."

"Last year," says Johan Muller of the Education Policy Unit at the University of the Witwatersrand, "you had anarchy in the classroom. Teachers were attacked, gangs developed, there was a dramatic increase in schoolgirl rapes. The webs of authority have been destroyed."

Monde Tulwana, a teacher at I D Mkhize secondary school in Guguletu township outside Cape Town, tells a similar story. "You've had hundreds of youngsters roaming the streets. They came when they felt like it, if they came at all. Gangsterism is rife in the townships and affects children who might want to come."

All this adds an extra edge to the reforms that might now begin to be negotiated. Having spent 40 years running an educational system whose chief purpose was to prevent blacks being educated, the regime is now looking for ways out of the crisis caused by its breakdown. That breakdown was brought on by insufficient funds, planning and resources, and exacerbated in recent times by protest strikes and boycotts by pupils to which the state's answer was to declare war, in effect, and send in the troops.

As a preliminary step — a one-off gesture to draw into the discussion the various existing education groups, including the ANC-connected National Education Coordinating Committee — the sum of R800 million (£182 million) has been proferred. To put that in context, the government estimates it would cost R5,200 million to bring black schools up to something like present white levels in terms of resources. The NECC estimates that it would take six times that figure.

As they face each other across the negotiating

table, Stoffel van der Merwe, the minister responsible for black education outside the homelands, and Ihron Rensburg, the General Secretary of the NECC, is each aware of the battleground — and in some cases it is literally a battleground — out of which they must find a path. The hard-faced footsoldiers just behind them are only too ready to blow the whole process sky-high if they don't like what's being given and what's being gained.

But the NECC also believes it is armed with a philosophy to which most blacks, Coloureds and Indians pay lip service, a belief on which the ANC negotiations with the government themselves are based — the idea that South Africa can be transformed into a non-racial, democratic society. And that of course involves, via the introduction of people's education, the transformation of the education system as well.

These impending discussions on education are a microcosm of the political negotiations that began in May in Cape Town. Some say that the crisis in black education was itself an important factor in forcing the government to take this historic step. Stoffel van der Merwe is on the government negotiating team at least in part because of the importance of the education issue.

The minister responsible for the Department of Education and Training — in apartheid-speak the man in charge of educating those blacks who do not live in the homelands — agrees that things must change. Stoffel van der Merwe has only been in the job since the last election. He is one of the new breed of white politicians who are willing to talk to ANC-associated black organisations about effecting change. Sitting in his office in a modern building next

LEARNING AND LOSING

to parliament in Cape Town, his view of the crisis sounds at times similar to that of the black educationists. "There are children in school who have no hope of passing their matriculation exams this year. For them school is an objectionable object, it is no use to them."

He and the government "recognise the present situation in black education is not acceptable. It is not as if we wish things to be as they are. We recognise that some classes are overcrowded, and that there are shortcomings, that there are colossal shortfalls."

The present system is better than nothing, he says, and strongly urges all parties to make use of it. "Even if they want to become terrorists, they will become better terrorists if they can count the number of bullets." But it soon becomes clear in conversation that he is looking at a way out of the present crisis that differs profoundly from that put forward by the NECC. He talks of liberalisation; they talk of democratisation. He wants change within the present political structure; they want people's education for people power. He wants to upgrade facilities and teacher qualification; they want that too — but they also want to re-educate the teachers out of the legacy of Bantu education introduced in 1950. He thinks in terms of ultimately raising black standards to the level of white standards; they see existing white standards themselves as a problem. The norms, according to this view, should be set at an attainable level lower than the present white standards but above the present ones set by the Department of Education and Training.

Stoffel van der Merwe argues that the present 15 education departments under a minister for national education offer movement towards a unitary system; they say that all these bureaucratic structures based on ethnic divisions must be scrapped. One single ministry responsible for policy for all races should be brought in.

Concerning the R800 million that he has offered to discuss with them, he makes the following point: "I want to involve them in decision-making on, for example, the quality of school buildings, and where they could be built. So, in a good neighbourhood, you might build a school costing R3 million whereas in a squatter neighbourhood you could build one costing only R1 million. I want their proposals. I would listen to anything so long as it is educationally accountable."

But he is not interested in discussing the "weirder ideas" of people's education

"I'm inviting them to come and negotiate a system for participation where the government will supply the means, the schools, train the teachers and pay them, and supply the infrastructure. But then the community must run the schools, they must appoint the teachers."

The NECC has other ideas. Their proposals may not surprise the minister, but they are unlikely to please his officials. Speaking in his modern office in Johannesburg, Ihron Rensburg suggests that the R800 million should go in two directions; for teacher re-education (which could also include upgrading), and for new schools (resources, materials, equipment and community libraries). This thrust is embodied in a national strategic plan that the NECC has prepared as the basis for further discussion.

It is also planning a campaign in the second half

of the year to open up more of the estimated 200 empty white schools. The government made a gesture of encouraging this by saying that if 90 per cent of parents voted in favour of allowing all races into a given school, they would be allowed to do so. Cape Afrikaner parents immediately threw a spanner in the works by rejecting even the possibility of discussing the 90 per cent option.

Stoffel van der Merwe says that this was a vote rigged by the far right and he isn't too concerned by it. More worrying in the wider context is that, while the Group Areas Act remains in force, schools would be unable to allow entry to children of another racial group even if they voted to.

Teachers are the target of everyone's efforts. Both sides regard them as crucial to the attempts to change the system. But the Department of Education and Training sees better pay and conditions, better training and qualification — and no real challenge to apartheid structures — as the way forward. The NECC wants to enlist them in the battle to overthrow those structures. So it certainly wants a say in their retraining, quite apart from their upgrading.

And that's where the real difference lies. Both sides are groping their way along a tightrope towards a goal which appears the same — a black education system that brings into some harmony the needs of whatever South Africa becomes and the demands of its black people. But their starting points and political ambitions are so far apart that there are dangers in even being seen on the same tightrope.

Stoffel van der Merwe has a department bred and nourished on the beliefs of apartheid which, as yet, are unchallengeable in educational terms. Quite apart from persuading blacks to work steadily for improvements within existing structures — even as they are seizing the political initiative for rapid change — he has to convince his bureaucrats to allow black ideas into curricula, teacher training, and finance. And that's without contending with the wider white electorate.

For the NECC, which obtains credibility by giving shape to aspects of the black liberation struggle, to be seen talking to Nationalist ministers and bureaucrats can easily lead to charges of collaboration. The students in the townships and the activists who mobilise them are not going to be easily satisfied with discussions on whether to build schools for R1 million or for R3 million. They want to see real progress towards people's education. Otherwise, many believe, they could start the process of strikes and boycotts all over again.

They are not easily swayed by authority, whoever it is. When Nelson Mandela told students to throw their weapons into the sea and go back to school, some of them showed their displeasure by cutting his face off their T-shirts.

The NECC also has a credibility problem with some educationists who say that they haven't done enough basic research on the nitty-gritty of replacing the present system. What kind of schools do you want? they are asked. And what exactly do you want taught in them, and by whom, and trained where?

Saleem Badat of the University of the Western Cape replies that they, like everyone else, haven't had enough time. They do not have the people to both mobilise for the struggle in the townships and do the necessary research. In some cases the same people have to do both. But he also indicates that the hard line is softening in the face of reality. He thinks they will get breathing space from the militants to try talking.

Ken Hartshorne believes that things will get worse in the next three to five years before they start to get better. This is because the euphoria surrounding Nelson Mandela's release, and F W de Klerk's willingness to talk, have increased expectations and simultaneously increased tensions. He sees the Cape Afrikaner rejection of open schools as an indication of this.

"It's easier for the government to release Mandela or scrap the Group Areas Act than to desegregate the education system. The challenges look very near now," he says. And adds that those pushing for people's education will be forced to temper their idealism.

Johan Muller is equally realistic: "No amount of tinkering by well-disposed ministers like Stoffel van der Merwe can go beyond what the logic and structures of his department allows. The system will just reproduce itself."

Ihron Rensburg has few illusions: "The relationship with the DET is about negotiation over crisis issues rather than resolving fundamental contradictions. But the minister knows the department cannot resolve actions like strikes and boycotts and so he has to negotiate with the NECC. But the bottom line is that whatever he concludes has to be referred back to the cabinet. So to some extent we are just going through the motions."

The minister has a very interesting gloss on the present state of affairs, stemming from a thesis he once wrote which he described as being about revolution as a phenomenon. He points out that revolutions explode when reforms have already begun. The way to manage such transformations, he suggests, is to keep tight control, keep expectations within manageable proportions and have reform "go hand in hand with a somewhat repressive security policy — not that I like that."

So, when offered this interpretation of that policy, he did not disagree: "We're going to beat you up because it's good for you in the long run."

The tightrope walkers will need to keep their heads.

PEOPLE'S education is the most radical response to the crisis. In its present form it grew out of the 1984-5 state of emergency, when troops were sent in to the classrooms and thousands of students were detained for protesting against the education system. It attempts to offer a grassroots, community-based alternative to state structures and philosophies.

People's education is linked with the liberation movement's aims, and is an attempt to work out the educational consequences of the Freedom Charter.

It has moved from its original vision of "Liberation now, education later" to "People's education for people's power". Even that formulation is constantly being rethought as the possibility of negotiating on educational spending, for example, becomes a reality.

It has a national and regional organisation in the National Educational Crisis Committee, based in Johannesburg and is building on research provided through Harold Wolpe's Research on Education in South Africa project at the University of Essex and its own education policy units at the universities of the Witwatersrand and Natal.

There are close links with the Congress of South African Trade Unions.

One of its purposes has been to channel the militancy of unorganised youth into disciplined action accountable to the whole community.

The basic educational objectives are:
- To eliminate illiteracy, ignorance, capitalist norms of competition, individualism, stunted intellectual development and exploitation;
- To enable the oppressed to understand the evils of apartheid, and to prepare them for participation in a non-racial democratic system;
- To equip and train all sectors of "our people" to participate actively and creatively in the struggle to attain people's power in order to establish a non-racial, democratic South Africa.

12 Internal exiles

Douglas Morrison

CHARLEY was a marked man. An activist at the height of the student protests in the mid-1980s, he was picked up by the police and detained on four separate occasions. The first three times they said to him when he came out: "We know who you are, you'd better watch out. You'd better leave town." Then, after the fourth time, they simply came to his cell and said they were letting him out. They were going to take him home to his parents. He didn't believe them, but he had to go with them anyway. They put him in a police van and drove out of town. When they came to a field, they stripped his clothes off, threw him out, and told him to run. Then they started shooting.

He ran and dodged and eventually fell down. Thinking they had hit him, or perhaps not really caring what became of him, they went away. After periods in hiding, the security authorities put it about that Charley had fled the country to be trained as a terrorist. He eventually found his way to the Interchurch Education Programme in Johannesburg. The IEP was set up in 1978 to help provide educational rehabilitation for young blacks whose schooling had been disrupted or ended by the upheavals of 1976. Many of its clients have been detained and kept in solitary confinement. Charley's story as he told it to them, is exceptional even for IEP. But, in the words of Sandy, one of the project workers, many of their students were "brutalised and become brutal themselves, angry, disruptive and uncontrollable, their own oppressors."

These are the real victims of the war that went on in 1985/6 around the schools for better education and control of the black townships. At its offices in a shabby six storey office block at the run-down end of the white business area, one IEP group of former activists agreed to talk about their experiences, although at the start they were extremely suspicious and hostile.

Quite apart from the treatment they received in prison — many were beaten or kept in solitary confinement — they were also threatened by the security forces when they came out. They say they were "marked out" for retribution, and as a result most state schools would not take them back.

They became what was known as "internal exiles", moving from house to house and from town to town. Their education was at an end, and, worse, they became virtually incapable of education. Hating authority and the discipline of education, and not trusting their teachers, who they saw as collaborators with the regime, or as people simply incapable of teaching or not perhaps wanting to teach.

Despite the claims of the state, they had not been

mobilised by "outside agitators", nor at the start were they acting from political motives. But once they'd been detained, all that changed. Most of them said that they were moved from police station to prison in different towns or different parts of the country. Their parents had been unable to find out from the authorities where they were. Most had been in solitary confinement. Some had been beaten. And there were always threats of what would happen when they got out.

They said that most detainees were asked to become informers. They were offered rewards, including instant release, money, cars, and housing. If the carrot failed, the stick might be employed to force them to accept. They estimated that one in five detainees collaborated to some extent.

Although the state of emergency has now been lifted from schools, they believe that the security forces are still infiltrating. Some claim to have recognised former interrogators turning up as new teachers, others say they have seen teachers in school with weapons tucked in their boots.

IEP tries to reintroduce them to the process of learning, initially by trying to get them to take part in and recognise the socialising and democratising process that can take place somewhere like a classroom. It also tries to persuade them to recognise that in education, students do not have the final say, that there is an authority which has legitimacy and which they have to accept.

The core of the programme is the tuition project which tries to help about 100 students a year towards matriculation. Although Christian in character, being largely funded by organisations like the World Council of Churches, and by German and Dutch church groups, it claims not to be evangelical. The IEP project, like others in the non state or alternate sector, has grown up to help those who cannot receive schooling in the state sector. So-called "street" schools, connected with the National Education Crisis Committee, have, according to Ihron Rensburg, its general secretary, up to 20,000 pupils. Private schools, allowed to be multi racial, have existed for some time, as have church schools.

Sandy believes that the damage caused by the crisis has hampered ways of solving it. "By banning student organisations and incarcerating their leaders, the state cut off the head, and compounded the problem of lack of control of gangs of militants. They also removed the channel for negotiations on ways to stop the strikes and violence.

"In the seventies, student leaders of Steve Biko's calibre provided an intellectual framework for channelling dissatisfaction. In the early eighties, organisations like the Congress of South African Students equally provided a leadership through which dissatisfaction could be channelled. Now they've got street gangs, who are not organised to negotiate."

After Charley came to IEP, they noticed an increase in what they suspected was security force interest in the students. Apprehension about infiltration is always there, and sometimes justified. Sandy said that two of their students had been detained when they went home in April.

And Charley? He was eventually accepted for a course at a Cape college where he became student president. When last heard of he was working down there.

13 Sickness in the system

Angella Johnson

BODIES are piling up in the mortuary of Soweto's Baragwanath hospital. Medicines are unavailable, dirty linen left unwashed, emergency surgeries cancelled and patients discharged early following strike action by non-medical workers.

Baragwanath, a teaching hospital under the auspices of the University of the Witwatersrand Medical School, Johannesburg, serves an estimated four million black people. It is the largest hospital in Africa and is so over-stretched patients often have to sleep on the floor. In the Johannesburg General, built in 1980 for white patients, about half the beds are empty.

Health care in Johannesburg, as in most of South Africa, has been beset by labour unrest, severe staff shortages and racial discrimination. The current crisis is merely a symptom of the general malaise created by apartheid policies and the growing number of black people moving into cities and needing medical care.

This, coupled with inadequate government funding, has precipitated a slump in morale. Frustrated doctors, nurses and other health workers are leaving the profession or moving into private practice. In white hospitals some wards are closed because of lack of staff, others due to a shortage of patients.

A changing South Africa is now questioning whether its increasingly crippled health services can continue with expensive First World treatment while the majority of its citizens live a Third World existence. Health care is still largely unequal and inadequate. Hospitals are legally segregated, there are serious inequalities in access to health care across urban-rural, white-black and rich-poor divides. Yet the country is reported to have more body scanners at R7 million (£1.6 million) each than Britain.

In Johannesburg about 500 people are on dialysis machines for kidney failure. That is higher than anywhere else in the country. But doctors in Baragwanath complain that their machines are so dated they could be dangerous to patients.

Professor John Milne, Dean of Wits Medical School, says that budgetary restrictions have made it difficult to keep updating machines. "Funds have only been provided to replace essential outdated and irreparable equipment. We are reaching a stage where we have to think of cutting the number of people who receive renal dialysis treatment, because it is becoming extremely expensive. "At the moment most people of all colours are able to get dialysis, but we are thinking of introducing an age limit because we cannot afford to maintain the present level of treatment. Looking to the 1990s there is no doubt that South Africa cannot continue with its emphasis on hi-tech treatment when people in the townships are more in need of basic primary health care."

The move towards improved primary care is driven by the economic and social needs of a large black under-class which has been badly served under apartheid. "We would like to reduce the number of teaching hospitals and replace them with a combination of clinics and smaller referral hospitals."

Such a system would include a number of clinics scattered throughout townships and elsewhere. People would be encouraged to use these and the general practitioner as the first means of contact before approaching a hospital.

Local care would include preventive medicine, promotion of good health and providing basic treatment for common ailments. Most doctors working in townships like Soweto and Alexandra insist that decent housing, education, good nutrition, ante-natal care, birth control, and sanitation are also important prerequisites for better health care.

At a recent medical seminar at the University of Stellenbosch Dr Rina Venter, the Minister for Health, gave her support for such a shift in policy. Cedric de Beer, co-director of the Centre for the Study of Health Policy, agreed there should be a move from a preference for the highly advanced to basic community-orientated health services: "What we are saying is that scarce or expensive resources will only be used where this is clinically cost effective. For example, penicillin will be used where more modern antibiotics are now often used with no greater therapeutic efficiency. "Desegregation of hospitals is not only a moral, but also an economic imperative. It is necessary forboth short term crisis management and long term rational planning."

But how does one cut the cake in order to provide

SICKNESS IN THE SYSTEM

social care and public health on a non-racial basis? Mr De Beer believes this can only be done by the introduction of a national health service running alongside a small private sector.

Things are changing rapidly, but the government still has a fragmented system of 14 different health ministries — including three Own Affairs departments dealing with Coloured, Indian and whites. The effects of apartheid will remain long after the installation of a democratic government. For instance, a disproportionate share of health resources have been invested in the white areas: a future health service will be faced with the problem of redistributing these resources to ensure blacks have access to equal care. A single, non-racial department of health will be faced with the problem of unifying all health workers and administrative structures.

At Baragwanath, the predominantly black general assistant staff are demanding a living wage, recognition of their union and better conditions of labour. Many kitchen, cleaning and security staff earn a minimum salary of R223 a month, which they want increased to R1,100.

The National Health and Allied Workers Union is also demanding shorter working hours and permanent employee status for it members, many of whom even after 20 years are still classified as temporary staff and liable to immediate dismissal. Thomas Mahori,38, is a shop steward and has worked in the stores at Baragwanath for 10 years. He earns about R600 per month and out of this looks after his wife and four children in Soweto and regularly sends money to his parents in Gazankulu, a black homeland in the northern Transvaal. He said: "I have to pay HP, rent, bills, and buy food from this tiny amount of money. I can't cope on what they pay me. That's why we are angry and decided to stop working. They say I'm a temporary worker and that's why the hospital can get away with paying me this amount of money."

The authorities are reluctant to recognise the union, because the resulting salary rises would stretch an already straining budget. Cutbacks have already led to plans for a new teaching hospital in Durban being frozen. In the Free State, where the health budget was only increased by 1 per cent to R434 million, the recent closure of 170 beds at two hospitals was blamed partially on the resignation of eight doctors in protest at the lack of funds. The Transvaal budget was increased by 0.8 per cent to R1.9 billion, following a year when the shortfall was about R242 million.

Doctors and medical aid agencies have warned that such cuts will put health care back several years, unless immediately stemmed. "Thousands of people — black and white — are being turned away from state institutions, or are on long waiting lists," said one Johannesburg doctor. Increasing numbers of those who can afford it, are being urged to resort to private medical aid. At a "crisis meeting" in Johannesburg, doctors from all over the country called on the government to implement major changes — including the official ending of apartheid in health and redistribution of funds to meet local needs.

[Since this was written the South African government has announced the ending of apartheid in health care.]

14 Pressing for change

Georgina Henry

CENSORSHIP and the intimidation, harassment, detention, seizure and fines that went with it has bred a particular kind of protest journalism in South Africa. Simply trying to record what the state wanted unrecorded has narrowed the focus of serious journalism and left it now endeavouring to interpret the opening-up of political debate.

The emergency media regulations were lifted, in the main, on February 2, although the police can still order journalists away from scenes of "unrest" and security action and pictures of these scenes cannot be broadcast or published without permission. But about 100 laws still impinge on the daily work of journalists by restricting the free flow of information in South Africa. The latest bulletin of the South African Anti-Censorship Group records the mixed signals still coming from the government: on the one hand increased tolerance for long-repressed views, on the other signals that the machinery of censorship remains in place if and when the government wants to use it.

While the case was going ahead against Vrye Weekblad under the emergency regulations — even though the relevant regulations had been lifted — for publishing six "subversive" statements about military conscription; another 47 names of people who may not be quoted had been removed from the Internal Security Act list.

The emergency media regulations failed to stifle dissent but left it marginalised in the "alternative" sector: a crop of independently owned titles with small circulations. But censorship is only one of the factors that has tamed much of South African journalism. The English press has been hit by the emigration of some of the brightest people. Black journalists have suffered from poor education and indifferent training on white-run newspapers.

This situation is exacerbated by the lack of competition among commercial newspapers. Anglo-American, the biggest mining house, ultimately owns the Argus Group and Times Media Ltd which together publish almost every English language daily and Sunday newspaper. Afrikaanse Pers and Nasionale Pers manage the commercial Afrikaner market.

The debate has already begun on to what press freedom, so abused under a white government, would mean under a black government. On the agenda are such issues as nationalisation, state subsidies, accountability to unions and the communities, a ban on "racist" language, and breaking the white monopoly.

Zwelakhe Sisulu, editor of New Nation, who is helping formulate ANC media policy, treads carefully. "That you own the most media does not make you the most effective communicator, as we have seen under the National Party," he says. He believes, however, it is legitimate for the state to own newspapers and television, so long as it does not serve sectarian party interests. "If you're going to use media as an eduction tool then it is important that the state owns a large section of the media, but that in no way will compromise other independent publications."

Irwin Manoim, the co-editor of Weekly Mail, who raised the issues on a recent trip to the US, and found his speech widely criticised by some South African newspapers says: "Public intervention in the media is legitimate, but it should take the form of neutral assistance for newspapers in distribution and printing rather than interfering with the press," he says.

Harvey Tyson of The Star says: "There has to be adjustment, and there is room for a free commercial press, and state and subsidised newspapers. But this must allow hostile newspapers as well as independent newspapers."

"There's a misconception that we don't have a free press here, but we have the freest press in Africa," says Max du Preez of Vrye Weekblad. "The fact we exist shows that. If you're prepared to fight for freedom you can do a hell of a lot.

"Personally I find the ANC a mature organisation as far as their attitude to criticism goes. If they come into power we will treat them as the government. We're on our guard against trends in the liberation movement who want to see severe curbs on press freedom, but it's too soon to judge."

"SO, WE HAVE the ANC guys coming in tomorrow for the talks. Will they be safe? What about Joe Slovo?"
"He's a communist, not a criminal".

"Yes, but there's still the suppression of communism law. It's been ineffective since February 2, but let's check. If they arrest him, there'll be trouble." Themba Molefe, political editor of The Sowetan, will write the story, and says he'll profile the delegation due to arrive at Jan Smuts airport the following morning.

But before the morning news conference of the biggest black newspaper in South Africa moves on, the news editor, Sello Rabothata, updates the reporters on Horatio Motjuwadi, the sports editor of The Sowetan. He has been held under Section 29 of the Internal Security Act since April 12, which means that no one has been able to see him. The news that morning is that he's in hospital with the heart condition that has plagued him for years. The Sowetan has run a story on him every day, but no one is quite sure why he's being held. There's speculation that it was part of a swoop on the black journalists' union, MWASA, since three other members of its executive, including the general secretary, have also been detained.

The Sowetan is owned by the Argus group, (and ultimately Anglo-American) and therefore its bottom line is to make money. This it is slowly beginning to do. But the problem for a black commercial newspaper, says Joe Thloloe, the deputy editor, is that as black politics are being more openly debated, the paper cannot afford to take sides. He says this reflects the belief of the editor and journalists rather than, as others say, a commercial pressure not to align too closely with the ANC.

"The problem with other newspapers is that they don't reflect the full spectrum of black politics," he says. "White papers like The Star (published by the same group) reflect white politics, and black politics are seen by whites as just the ANC and nothing else. We have tried to look at black politics from (Chief Buthelezi's) Inkatha through to the PAC (Pan-Africanist Congress) and Black Consciousness. That means we've run into trouble when the UDF (United Democratic Front) and Cosatu (Congress of South African Trade Unions) tried to organise a boycott of The Sowetan at the height of the unrest. They didn't succeed though."

The Sowetan holds a special place in the history of black journalism in the country. It grew out of The World (banned in 1977) and The Post (closed in 1981), and suffered for years because its title had been that of the "knock and drop" (free-sheet) distributed by The Post in the township. Since it became a real newspaper in 1981 it has struggled to be a worthy successor to The World and The Post.

For the large number of black journalists who worked on the newspaper's predecessors, it was considered *the* place to be when unrest swept through the townships in the mid-1970s. Black journalists were able to go where their white colleagues were not. Thloloe — who worked on The World and The Post and was detained for 18 months between 1977 and 1978 — says this was when the black editors became more than just token in a white-managed newspaper.

The Black Consciousness culture is still there, which is why The Sowetan's relations with the pro-ANC paper, New Nation, appear strained; why Thloloe talks of the importance of reflecting a wide range of black political opinion; and why there's not much written about whites.

The Sowetan's black critics say it runs too many

stories about the PAC and not enough about the ANC; playing down last week's talks, for instance, since the PAC opposes negotiation. The story about the arrival of ANC delegates, ended up on page four. Some black journalists left the paper because of what they saw as a divisive trend in the liberation movement. Thloloe says he is trying to run a newspaper and not a party organ, but agrees that he is a PAC supporter.

So is Molefe. "The major problem we have now that the ANC is unbanned, is that people think we're against them. But right now a black commercial newspaper is committing suicide if it takes sides." As the paper's political editor, he says his role is to report extra-parliamentary politics. Black journalists were not allowed into the press gallery until a couple of years ago when the tri-cameral parliament was created, and The Sowetan has decided not to take up a place. "Too much real news is happening outside parliament," he says.

He considers himself black first, then a journalist. "Most people here are not ANC supporters. I'm PAC because they're talking the language of liberation. I'm not anti-white. The PAC doesn't believe in colour but in loyalty. But I do believe that not enough journalists are analysing the shifting changes in black politics."

For all this, the politics of the journalists appear rather watered-down in The Sowetan. "I don't know if I would automatically equate the stridency of the alternative media with being radical," says Thloloe. "We're as rigidly opposed to oppression and injustice as New Nation, but we're in favour of everyone who opposes this."

His editorial that day was on the political violence in Natal. "The attention of the world has been focused on the violence between Inkatha and the UDF/Cosatu alliance in Natal," he wrote. "The violence between the other organisations has been conveniently forgotten or ignored . . . With the unbanning of the ANC, the PAC, and other organisations, there is now strong competition for members. If the leaders of political organisations and their followers do not address the violence it will only escalate with the competition. Liberation means much more than getting the vote. It means freedom of speech, freedom to debate issues without fear of assualt or death. The organisations should see that their followers do not make the struggle for liberation hollow."

The Sowetan claims a readership of 1.2 million and a daily sale of 196,000. Advertising is looking healthier than for years, but the paper is still hampered by lack of resources. There is one computer terminal for every three journalists.

And the legacy of poor black education and writing (in a second language) skills, censorship, and lack of competition among newspaper groups mean the newspaper is slight on analysis and hard reporting. It's a tabloid for "the man in the street," says Thloloe. "I always dream of running a publication like the Weekly Mail but no one will buy it. We're not directed at middle-class whites."

AT NEW Nation, Zwelakhe Sisulu is still relishing the sensation of being back in an editor's chair frequently denied him by detention and banning orders since the newspaper started in 1986. The delight he takes in preparing that week's front page — with pictures of ANC secretary-general Alfred Nzo, South African Communist Party secretary-general Joe

Slovo, and two other ANC national executive members — is obvious. De Klerk's February 2 speech, which made this possible, is a vindication for the paper and its ANC politics, he says.

But Sisulu, son of the recently liberated Walter Sisulu, is also reassessing the role of the newspaper and himself as editor. "This new situation calls for some changes. In the past, the issues of struggle and of resistance were almost exclusively our terrain in the alternative media. Not any more. Now we have an opening-up of a society, and all of these things are fair game.

"It's ironic that the alternative media who have striven so hard for the new set of conditions, are now finding we have to change because we do not have the capacity to compete with the mainstream papers, who are now covering these kind of issues without fear of government intervention."

New Nation, however, *is* the voice of the ANC and the UDF, and Sisulu's own role in the movement has blurred the lines between editor and political activist. Since Mandela was released Sisulu has acted as a cross between a press officer and a personal assistant for the ANC's deputy president. He has organised the hundreds of interviews, the press conferences, the rallies, and is playing a central role in defining the ANC's media policy as one of the five-member executive within the National Reception Committee.

Within weeks, he promises, he will choose between the two roles, and that of editor will triumph. "I cannot do justice to both functions. But for the past few months the movement has been in transition. Anyway, it hasn't given New Nation favoured status with the ANC. In fact, there are certain things I can't pass on, which means the newspaper has been beaten to some stories."

But the paper's political colours will not change. "I do not believe one must simply say we must not take sides. But if one does, one has to be able to defend one's association. And as far as I'm concerned the ANC has a set of political principles and a political programme that is superior to everything else this country has to offer. But if we reached the point where this equation no longer stood, certainly we would distance ourselves."

The difficulty for New Nation is to engineer this shift to the centre of the debate without compromising its politics. To some extent, the shift has begun because the ANC itself has moved to centre stage. New Nation's circulation has risen to 75,000, perhaps as a reflection of this, but it is a long way from being financially independent. Owned and published by the South African Catholic Bishops Conference, it is heavily subsidised: its editorial budget is about R2.8 million a year (about £600,000) its income from advertising and sales about R600,000 (£136,000).

In the few weeks since he's been back at the paper, Sisulu has commissioned a team of management consultants and a market research company to advise him how to position the newspaper and help it to become financially self-sufficient. He is preparing to capitalise on new attitudes from advertisers reluctant to be seen to support the newspaper in the past.

He also aims to improve the training of black journalists. This, he says, is a fundamental problem for the black press. Too often, black journalists bring back the stories from the townships only to have them moulded into newspaper English by a white sub-editors desk. "For years we have had black reporters who major in English at university but whose command of the English language is not on a par with the people who have grown up speaking it. We won't really see serious black journalism until this is redressed. It's not laying out the paper that's a problem, it's the command of the language. Even at New Nation we have a bottleneck, with a newsroom and a small subs desk where every sentence and every paragraph must be gone through. The training programmes at the moment are pretty useless, including ours by the way."

A CLASSIC Ken Owen column in April quoted Dylan Thomas and Alan Paton in its fiery denunciation of the violence in Natal. "Our moral senses, like our public institutions, have been profoundly corrupted both by apartheid and by the struggle against apartheid," he thundered, before going on to take calculated and vicious swipes at the "moral ambivalence" of the likes of Bishop Tutu and Winnie Mandela, and those who ignored violence when it stemmed from the ANC or UDF.

It's this kind of column that has earned Owen, the editor of Business Day, the reputation as a maverick. In the weeks since the ANC has been unbanned, he has consistently criticised the calls for continued armed struggle, statements about nationalisation, and the ANC's inability to stop the violence. A letter in the paper complained that he had a blind spot when it came to Chief Buthelezi. Owen, who indulges himself with personal replies to correspondents, wrote: "My objection is to what I perceive as a systematic campaign to exonerate the UDF/ANC by blaming Inkatha. I am not aware that Chief Buthelezi has ever exhorted his followers to violence. It is, after all, the ANC and its supporters who advocate armed struggle."

The front page of Business Day, voice of liberal white capital in Johannesburg, is an uneasy mix of impenetrable stories about the Reserve Bank and necklacing in Natal. Owen personifies his constituency in the sense that he believes the English commercial press is caught, politically powerless, between Black and Afrikaner.

"We're on the wrong side of both major political constituencies. We can't join the blacks and we can't join the Afrikaners. I believe we are landed with an enormous responsibility for what happens in this country, without the slightest capacity to influence the outcome. That's the crisis of the English commercial press. It's lapsed into frustration, posturing, irrelevant behaviour, and the inability to charter an editorial strategy which meant anything. Any political party you chose was likely to be wiped out at the next election."

This is not a problem that Owen believes he has himself. "I try to act as the standard liberal voice in the British rather than the American sense."

Owen treats his columns as a bit of an indulgence, based on some research he saw years ago which said only 7 per cent of readers dipped into editorial columns. "I treat the editorial space with a reckless scorn that no other editor in this country does," he boasts. "I say what I like, I change my mind, apologise, make mistakes, correct them. Now everyone reads them. But at least I know what I'm for, when the others only know what they're against."

Owen's writing — some of the classiest in the English language press — saves him from total vilification by his colleagues. But there is resentment because Business Day was Times Media Ltd's "safe" replacement of the Rand Daily Mail, whose demise in 1985 is still bitterly discussed by journalists. He says his political line is his own, and not the result of pressure from his owners who are, of course, ultimately Anglo-American.

One of his bugbears is the standard of journalism. On the one hand he scorns the lack of political direction he sees around him in the months since February 2: "It was easier to have Uncle Mandela inside." On the other, he is obsessive about the collapse in journalistic disciplines, which he blames on a combination of emigration, appalling mismanagement of the commercial companies — although he says this has changed — low status, bad pay, and in the case of black journalists, poor education. But he employs hardly any black journalists.

Legal restrictions on journalists have been exaggerated, he believes, but they have taken their toll in terms of confidence. "This is a brutal environment for journalists to work in. Take a young American or British journalist: he'll call up anyone and say look, I've got a question. My staff go through agonies of saying, how do I get in, what will he say, how should I ask the question and shall I write it down first."

AT THE STAR, the biggest selling daily newspaper in South Africa, Harvey Tyson is more positive about his role in the changing country, and about that of the press in helping to bring about change.

None of the commercial press is prepared to shout

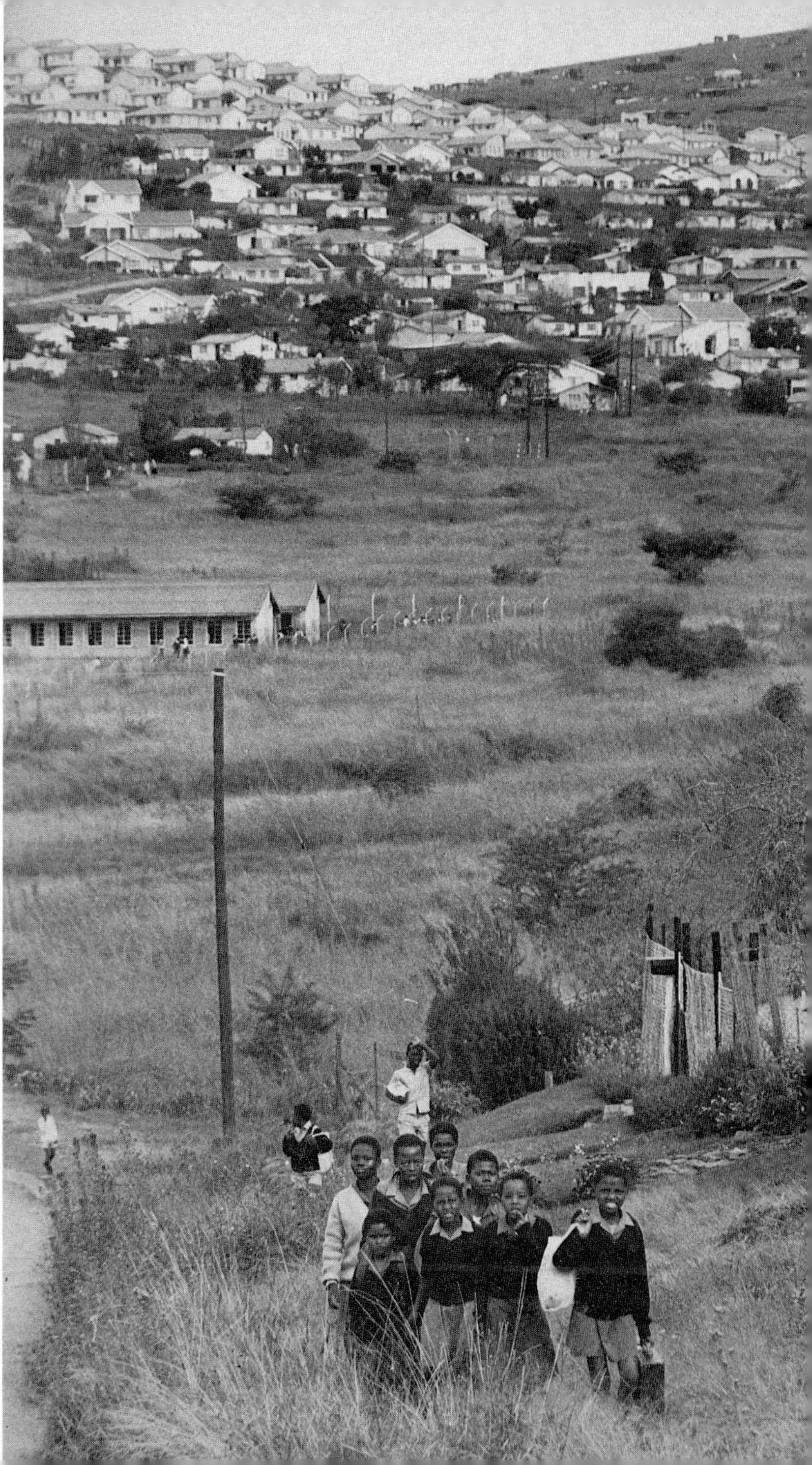

Black and white against apartheid
Previous page: Coming home from school in Natal

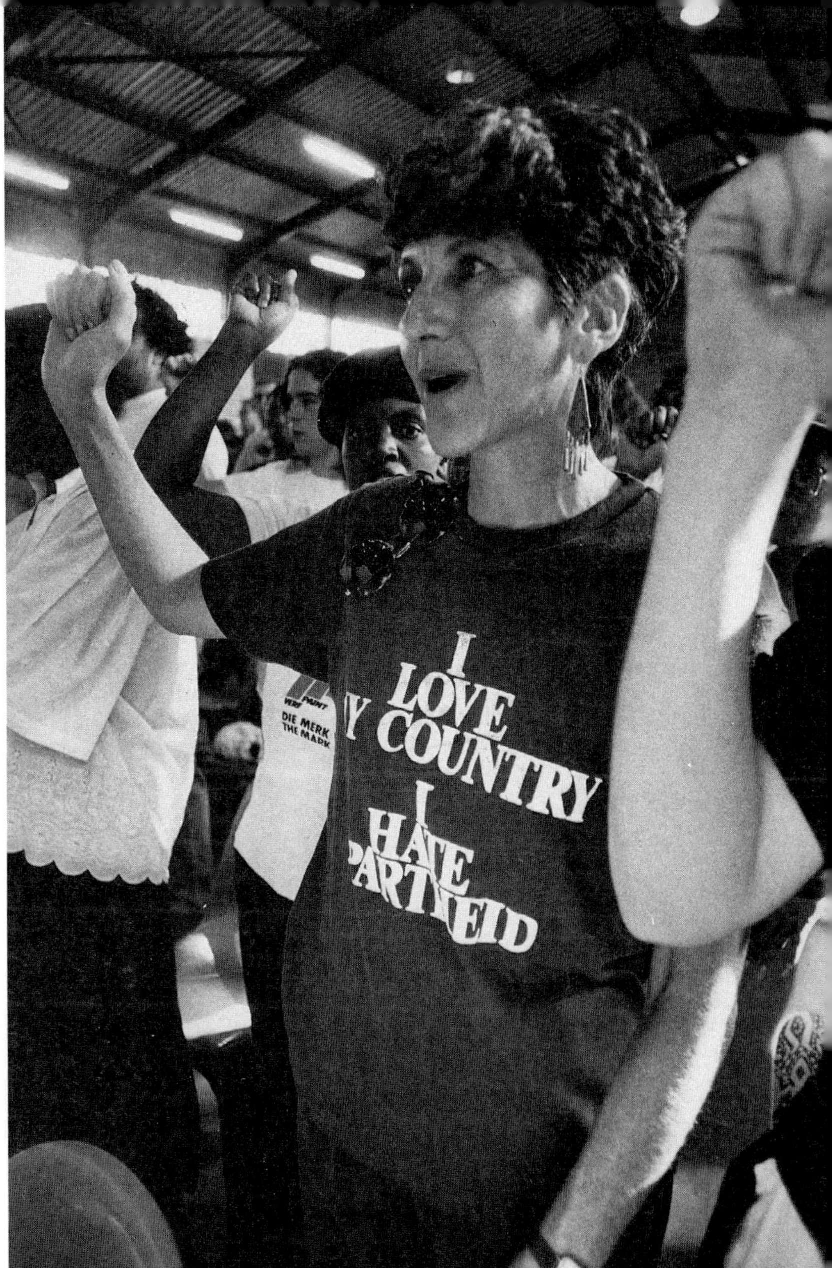
I
LOVE
COUNTRY
I
HATE

Leaving work in the rain, Orange Free State

Township Fever at the Market Theatre, Johannesburg

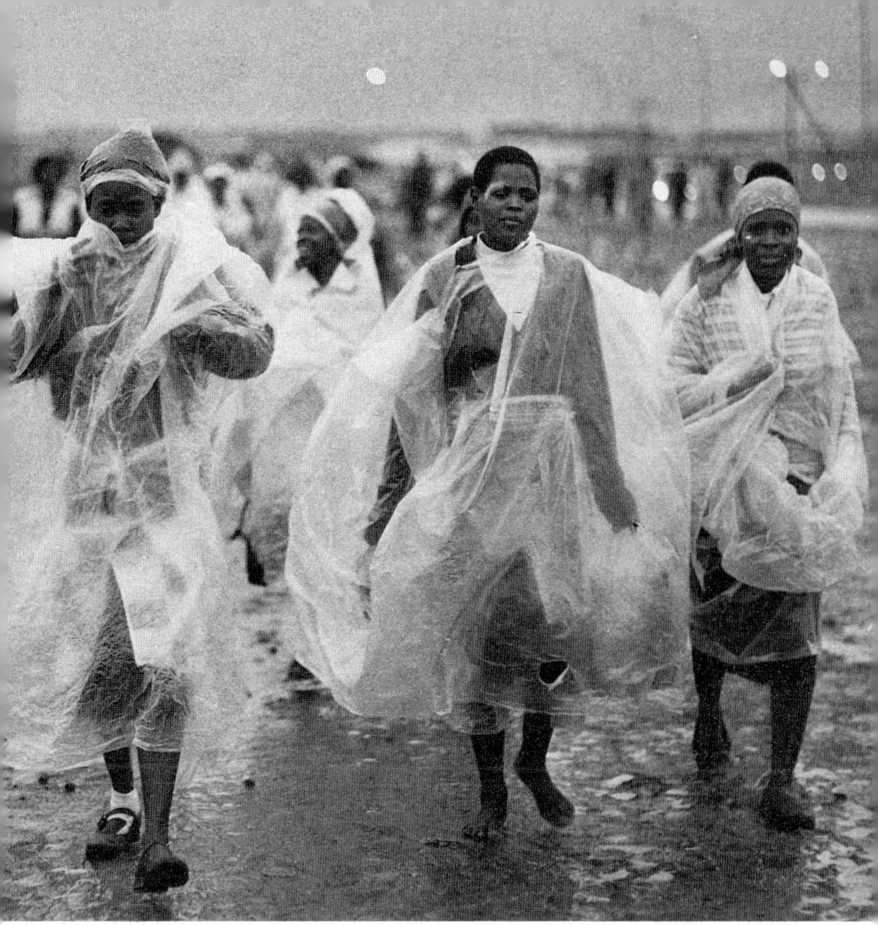

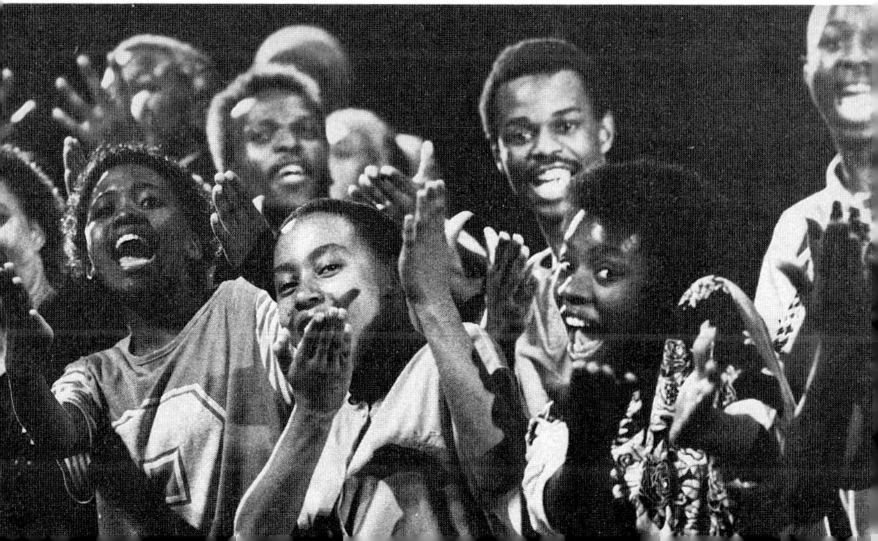

Tent city, Orange Free State

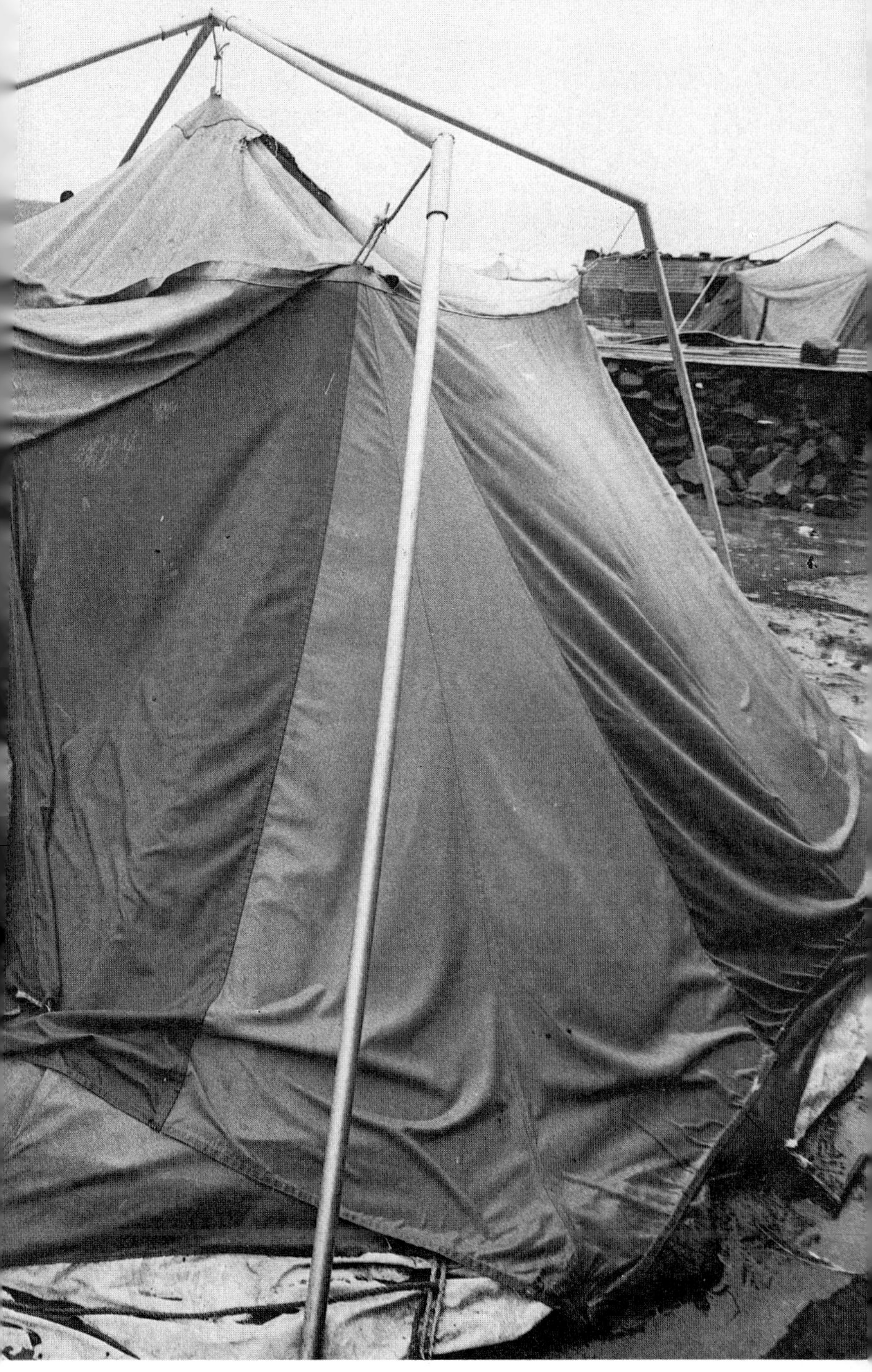

Beware of the gun: Private
security guards (above) and
a well-protected home (right)

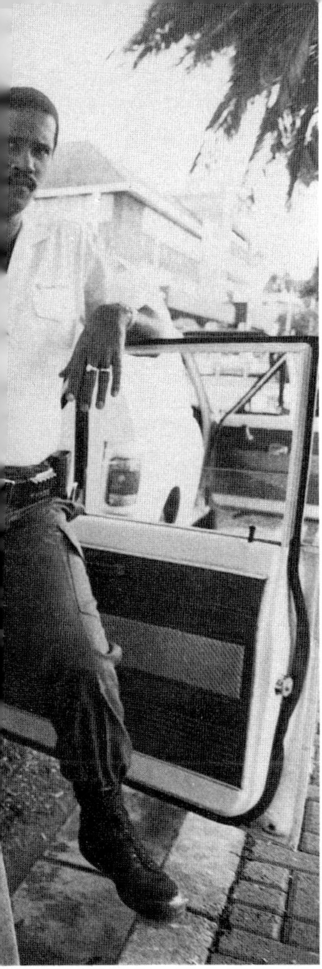

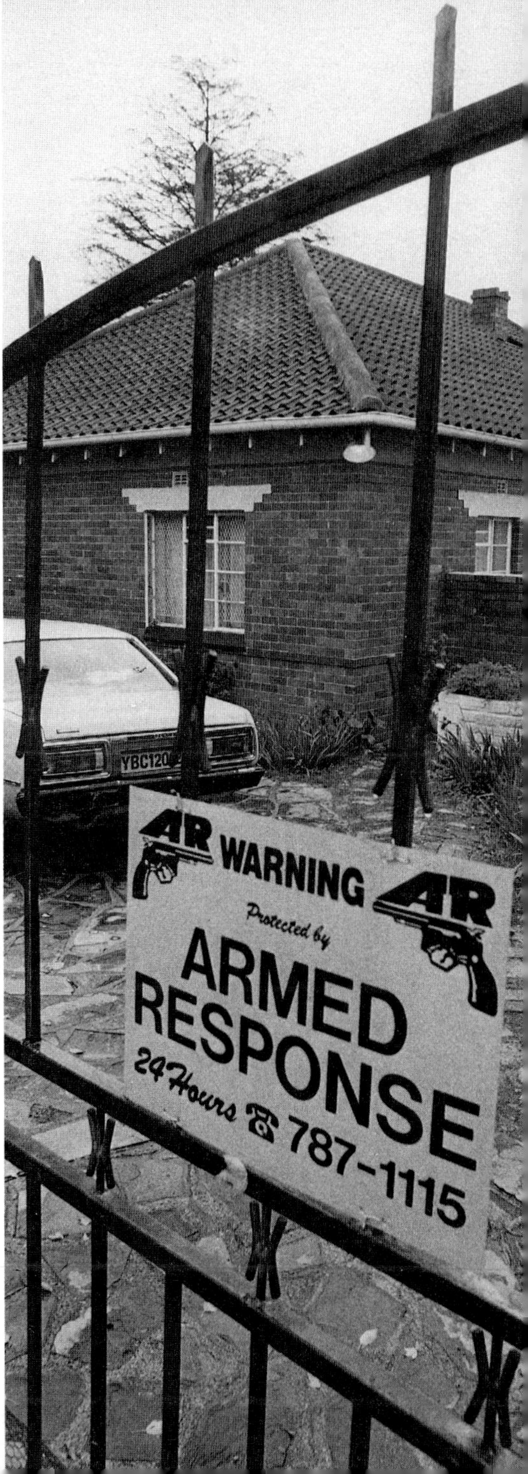
AR WARNING AR
Protected by
ARMED
RESPONSE
24 Hours 787-1115

Seeing eye to eye: apparent racial harmony in the streets of Johannesburg — but the scene was set up specially for a television commercial

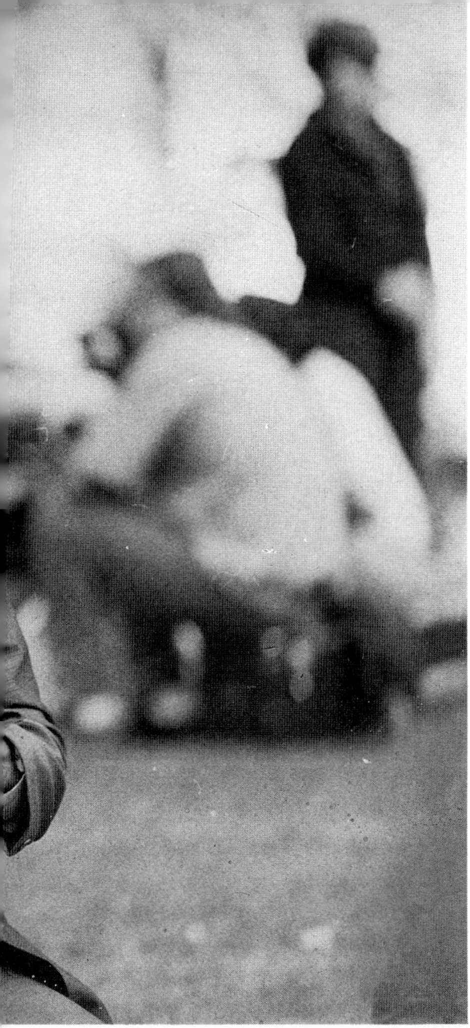

Looking the other way: reality in the streets of Johannesburg

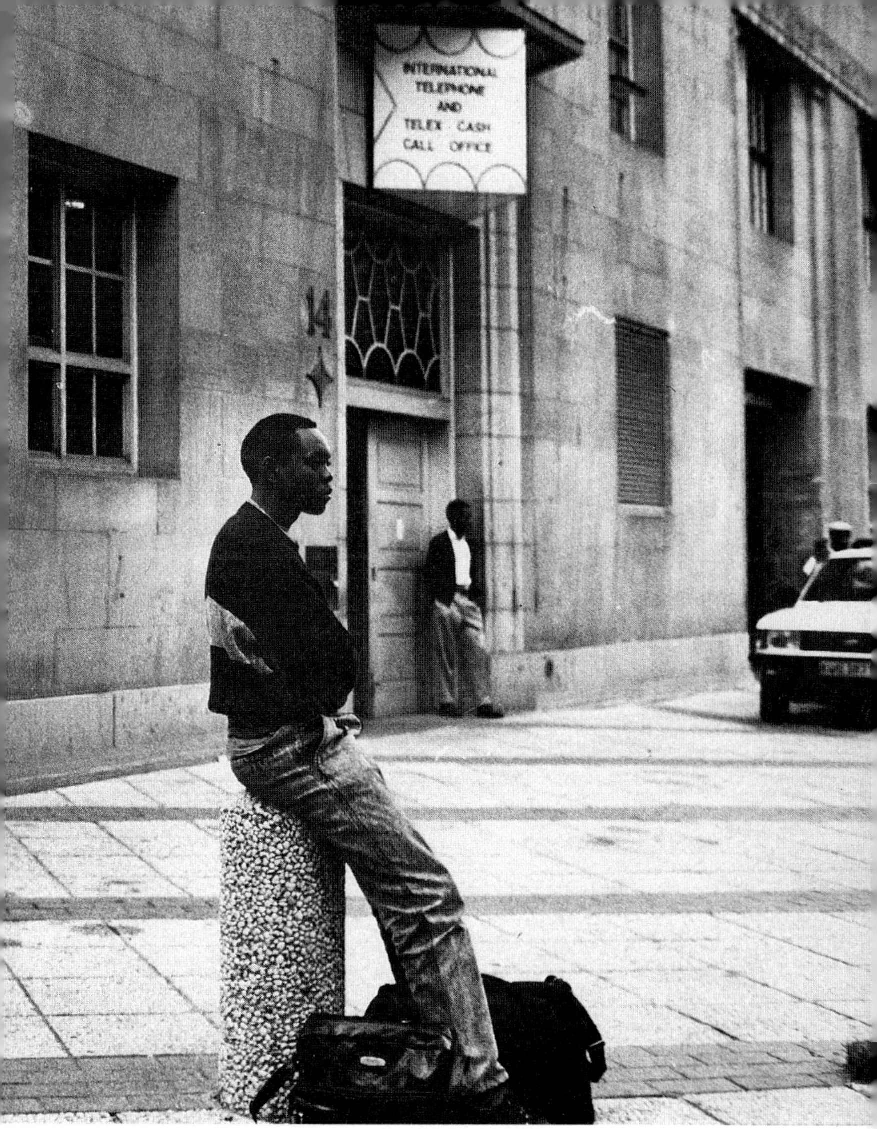
INTERNATIONAL
TELEPHONE
AND
TELEX CASH
CALL OFFICE
14

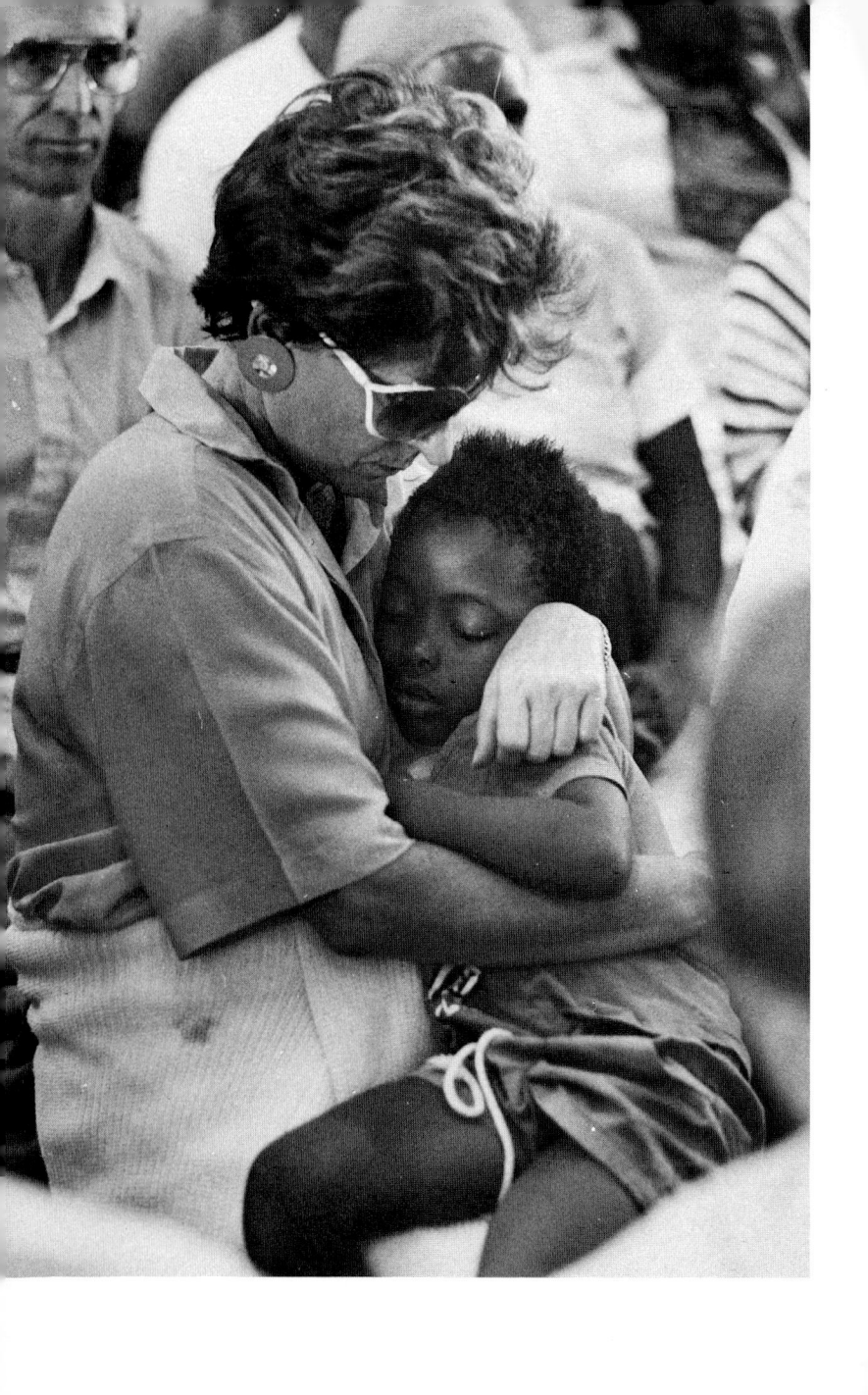

Face of the future: breaking down the barriers

Face of the past: statue of Paul Kruger, Afrikaner hero

Collecting instant rand, Johannesburg

Driving the cattle, Orange Free State

Es'kia Mphahlele, doyen of black South African writers, in Soweto

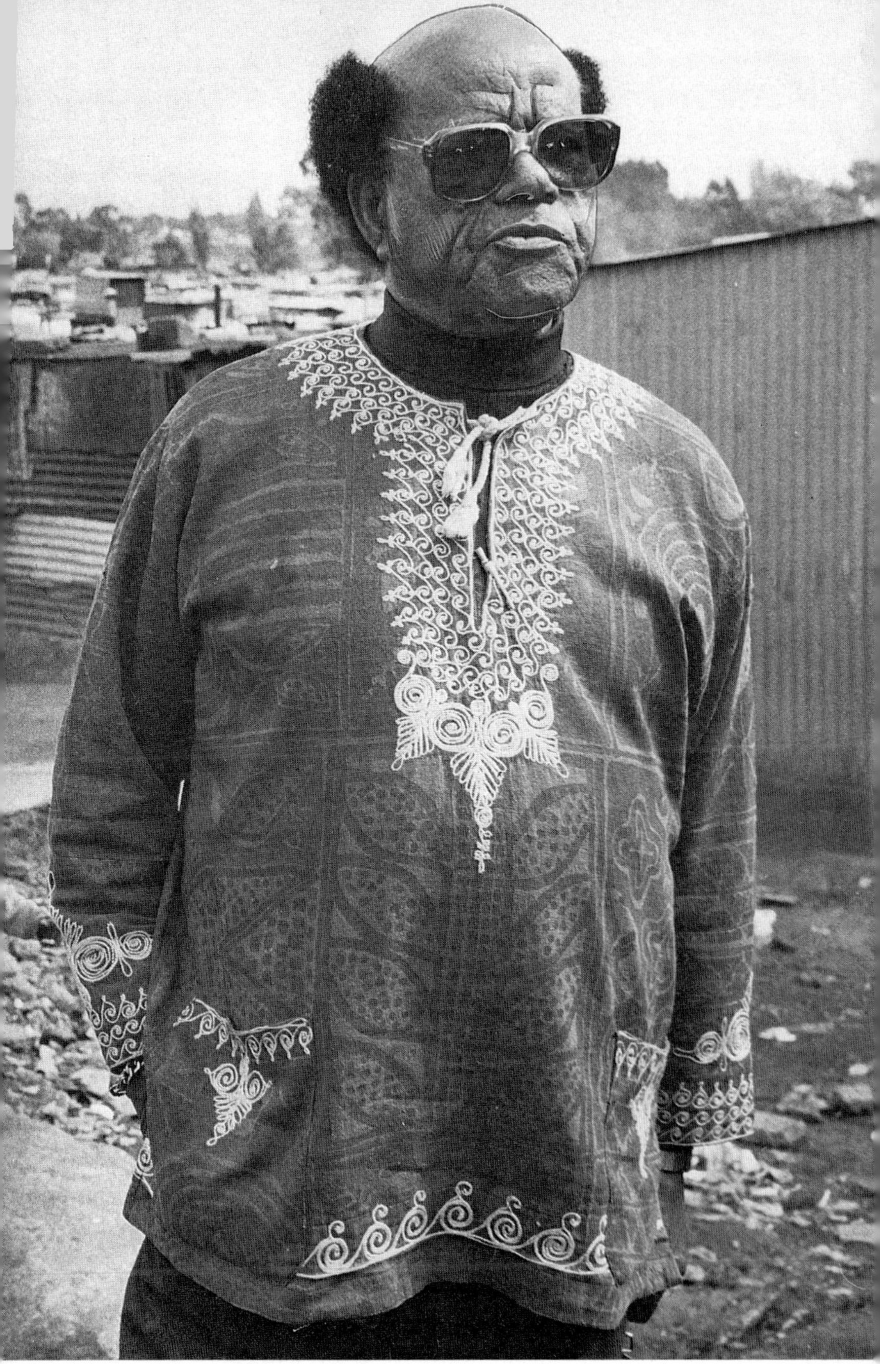

The textbook store at Vukukhanye primary school outside Cape Town. Because of neglect, six of its 16 classrooms are unusable.

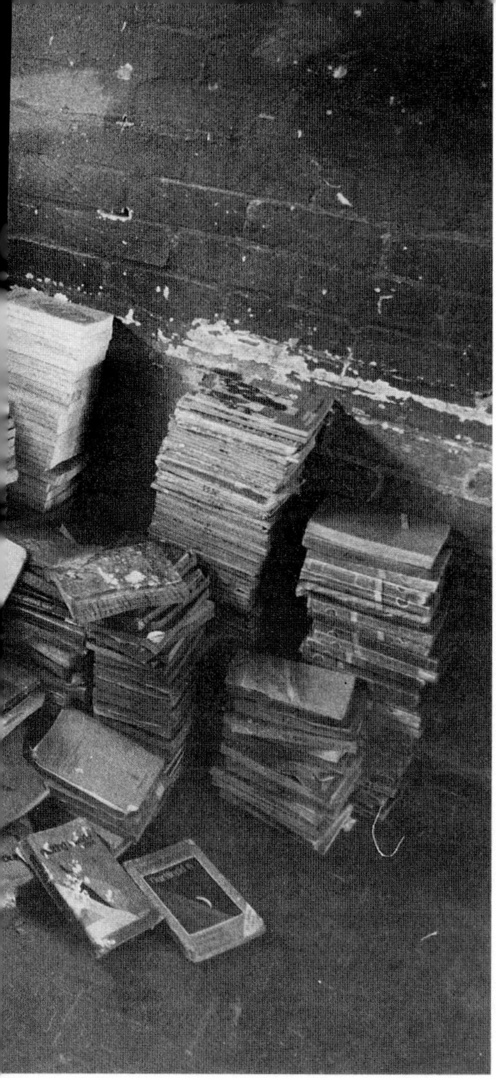

Road to riches? Gambling the night away in Sun City

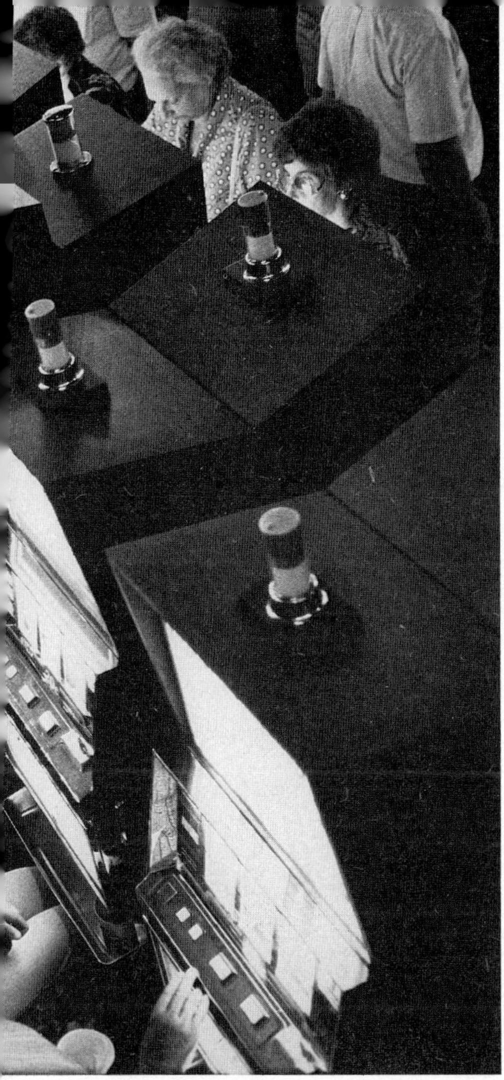

"Whites only" at the bus stop in Pretoria

wholeheartedly for the ANC, but The Star, 60 per cent of whose 250,000 readers are black, is sympathetic. "We can't go on shouting that capital is a good thing," Tyson says. "We have to find a middle way, which means taking into account nationalisation to some degree, and finding some forms for redistribution of wealth. We would go along with the ANC's view that there has to be a major adjustment of economic and social structures. We say, let's see how easily it can be done without destroying wealth, how it can help create wealth. I think liberally moderate would be the way to describe us."

Tyson, as the alternative press would say, is no radical. But he — with Max du Preez of Vrye Weekblad — has just been awarded the South African Society of Journalists award for press freedom. And he's had more problems than Ken Owen working under the emergency regulations: the citation recognises not only his own paper's role in reporting under the restrictions, but also his support for the alternative press who suffered far worse. "Flag-waving," Owen would grumble.

Breaking the law and showing strong political affiliation are precarious paths for the commercial press from an advertising and ownership point of view. And the intertwining relationship between Argus and Times Media has limited competition and, arguably, quality. Tyson says The Star, an evening paper but with eight editions, decided not to officially enter the morning market after the Rand Daily Mail closed in order to give Business Day — in the other group — a chance and see as many papers as possible survive.

The Star is one of the better newspapers in the

English language commercial press: while it mixes politics with populist gossip, its analysis is not bad and it carries more stories. But there are curiosities, like its separate editions for blacks in Soweto and whites in Johannesburg. If you approach a street seller and ask for an edition with a red map of Africa in the corner (the black edition), he will sell it to you, as a white, with the greatest reluctance. The black edition contains more stories about life in Soweto, educational material, and invariably leads its sports pages on soccer rather than rugby. Tyson says it's a commercial decision, not newspaper apartheid. "We'd love not to do it but the black readers want it."

THE GREAT hope for the English-speaking left lies in the birth in May 1990 of the new paper — probably to be called the Daily Mail — from the Weekly Mail team, whose founders and joint editors, Anton Harber and Irwin Manoim, both formerly worked for the Rand Daily Mail. This is the success story of the alternative press, hoping to claim its place in the mainstream of shifting politics. The venture which has raised R5 million (£1.14 million) from sympathetic backers, will be a public company with a staff trust controlling one-third of the shares and no shareholder owning more than 15 per cent.

The Weekly Mail's news conference is discussing the impending talks in Cape Town. Harber wants a personalised piece on the returning exiles. "Is it time to have a close look at the PAC, see what kind of support they've got now," asks a reporter. The week before there had been a fierce debate about the paper's attitude to the ANC. Harber had queried whether it was being objective enough, even though it was the

Weekly Mail which broke the story about the murder of Stompie Moeketsi, allegedly by Winnie Mandela's bodyguards.

Moving into the mainstream, however, will not dilute the newspaper's oppositional stance. Since 1985 it has been the leading radical anti-apartheid weekly, prosecuted so often (almost all ultimately unsuccessfully) the editors have lost count. "We existed for a special reason, protest journalism, and the time for that is not over yet," says Manoim. "But it is ending, and we don't want to be left out on the fringes as a media irrelevancy, but to broaden our coverage. Not only are we moving centre stage, but the centre stage is moving towards us." The newspaper would be foolish, he says, to water down its politics. "The Star is becoming more liberal by the day and we can't afford to be a clone of The Star."

Advertisers who initially didn't want to know are beginning, finally, to rethink racial readership classification and prove their non-racial credentials, although it has been a long struggle. "It's a political argument as well as a commercial one," says Manoim. "The country has changed dramatically in the last six months and it is time for advertisers to radically rethink their concept of South African readership. In Johannesburg, for instance, black people have moved into white areas and there are parts in the centre of the city which are now 80 per cent black. It's an indication of the advertising industry's lack of interest in charting these changes that so little research has been done in this area."

Harber and Manoim conservatively estimate to match the Weekly's 30,000 circulation for the Daily. It will still be a tiny operation with an initial staff of 45.

The average age of the Weekly Mail's journalists is late-20s. "You simply can't expect newspapers here to match Fleet Street," says Manoim. "There's been a massive brain drain which has hit every profession in the country. We've got good black journalists but they've come through an educational system deliberately designed to de-educate. The kind of black people who succeed here have usually gone to private schools."

DIE BEELD advertises itself as the biggest Afrikaans daily: 364,000 white readers, the brochure proclaims. Its editor, Salie de Swardt, says he's a bit embarrassed by the slogan. "It looks so racial." So it will change, in the sense that it is to be promoted to advertisers as having readers in the high-income groups, which is the same thing as saying white.

In the changing times, it's all a matter of *how* you say things, but it's also the reality. More blacks than whites speak Afrikaans, but not many read Beeld or its sister papers in the Nasionale Pers group. Those who do must be amazed by the frequent mentions and full-colour photographs of Mandela and the "white pariah", Joe Slovo.

De Swardt is not an Afrikaner ideologue and his paper, when compared to Die Burger in the Cape, has been consistently to the left in terms of National Party politics. But it is a long way from being an opposition paper; "lojale verset" (loyal resistance) is probably the most appropriate description.

James McClurg, The Star's ombudsman who writes a weekly review of the Afrikaner press, puts Beeld in the lead. "The men who run these newspapers are not visionaries," he wrote. "Some have succeeded better than others in the heart-piercing process of discarding the myths and visions with which Afrikanerdom has long encumbered its sons. That they have succeeded at all, given the pressures to which they have been subjected, is a mark of courage."

Followers of the Afrikaans press say that at no stage has it pushed for reforms that have not already been mooted within the National Party. The party has used it to test the ground for ideas such as the release of Mandela — called for by Beeld in 1988 — and the review of the Group Areas Act.

Beeld asked for and received permission to publish an interview with Joe Slovo a few days before he was unbanned. "We are a strong supporter of De Klerk now," says de Swardt. "We are trying to help him to get to the negotiating stage, and to do more and to try to create a new democracy. We've been a supporter of the National Party but a critical supporter."

It was a delicate problem to reach the stage of pushing for negotations with the ANC. "When the Afrikaner community regarded, and still regards, the ANC as little more than a terrorist group, it is very difficult to get across a message that they are also politcally motivated and should be listened to."

Beeld and its sister papers are an important support for De Klerk's moves to reform. De Swardt's view about the basis for political negotiations, for instance, could have come from the mouth of De Klerk himself. "I don't see power-sharing as opposed to majority rule. I'm all for majority rule, but with certain checks and balances. We are using our opinion pages, and we are looking at lots of different models.

"The debates are about the fundamental things:

what is a democracy; what is majority rule; what do checks and balances mean; what about constitutional concepts like proportional representation; to what extent does Germany have majority rule and Britain not?"

But the mainstream Afrikaans press is also trying to discredit the far right and, in some instances, is chipping away at Nelson Mandela, which helps to lend credence to other black movements like Inkatha. "Nelson's honeymoon is over", said a Beeld front-page headline early in April, backed by a report that there were signs of conflicting factions in the ANC and that it might not be fully prepared for the talks with De Klerk.

De Swardt says there is no deliberate strategy, but adds: "If the moderate people, the right wing of the ANC, were to subscribe to the normal sort of Western values that we believe in . . . instead of some of the strange things that they're thinking about on the left wing . . ." The seed has been planted.

BUT Beeld's loyal support for De Klerk has not gone down well with all its readers, and Z. B. Du Toit ("call me Z B"), editor of Die Patriot which is based at Conservative Party headquarters in Pretoria, says he has been the beneficiary. The Conservative Party — the official parliamentary opposition with 41 seats — is raising R20 million to launch a commercial weekly, probably a Sunday, and Du Toit is running a competition in his newspaper to choose a name, though does not yet know if he will be its editor.

"I'm like Pravda. I'm absolutely the mouth-piece of the Conservative Party," he says of his paper, for which he claims a weekly sale of 25,000. It roughly breaks even, with advertising support from Conservative-controlled councils, holiday resorts, and so on.

"Actually I consider myself part of the alternative press; I'm just at the other end of the spectrum. But now I am telling you that the majority of Afrikaners would support the Conservative Party, so that's why the party is launching a commercial paper. We too are moving mainstream since De Klerk has been talking to Mandela."

In an attempt to attract support from English-speaking right-wingers, Die Patriot runs two English pages. More and more vociferously it is promoting the concept of a separate Afrikaner homeland and trying to undermine De Klerk. "If ever there were reasons to adopt the policy of partition," a recent commentary proclaimed, "it is the constant sight of pictures of dancing, fist-clenching blacks shouting the odds about so-called grievances . . . Who needs it?" Our interview was interrupted by an English-speaking woman who rushed into the room to deliver a letter denouncing De Klerk's latest speech.

Du Toit was congratulating himself on his latest issue whose splash was a secret report by a National Intelligence Service spy who alleged that the ANC was preparing to assassinate right-wingers. Du Toit is unlikely to be prosecuted although he boasted that, under the law, publication of the document carried a 10-year sentence and R20,000 fine.

He genuinely believes that the way forward for Afrikaners is a separate homeland where no blacks would be allowed to live, and he is prepared to give up most of country's economic riches rather than live under a black government. "This we are floating in our letters column," he says. "We should do what we wanted the blacks to do. We'll leave Johannesburg, for example, for Azania."

AT THE other end of the Afrikaner press lies Vrye Weekblad, (Independent Weekly) the most prosecuted newspaper in South Africa precisely because it is the only Afrikaans paper to challenge white rule from the left.

Its editor, Max du Preez, a refugee from the commercial Afrikaans press — 11 years with Beeld — holds particular contempt for his former colleagues. "They *hate* us," he says with satisfaction, "and that's because we write about them as well. You have to realise that an anti-apartheid Afrikaans newspaper is a contradiction in terms. We are seen as fundamentally treasonable, and against everything that is holy about Afrikanerdom.

"We have a tradition here. When you are an Afrikaner and you turn against apartheid, you normally become anglicised. Well I'm most definitely not. I'm from good farming stock in the Free State, a rural boy, and they hate that.

"I started Vrye Weekblad because I know that my father and my uncles and my cousins are from rural areas, and I know they are fine people. But they are also racists, and they do the most appalling things, and they vote for the National Party. It has become clear to me that they simply don't know what is going on in this country. There's been a massive conspiracy of silence. We always had the English press, but when they wrote about the things that were going on, the excuse in Afrikanerdom was that it was the poisonous English press."

Vrye Weekblad has a circulation of only 13,000,

which does scant justice to its importance. As he sat calmly sucking his pipe, Du Preez faced a R1 million rand libel writ from the deputy commissioner of police, a R500,000 writ from "super-spy" Craig Williamson and another R200,000 writ from P.W. Botha, all stemming from the revelations about South African hit-squads. He was due to appeal soon against a six-month suspended sentence and large fine for quoting Joe Slovo when he was still a banned person. He has lost his right to vote because of it. His defence rests on 200 press clippings from other papers also quoting Slovo, but they picked on Vrye Weekblad because its an Afrikaner newspaper. Similarly, when the newspaper started in 1988 it cost him R30,000 (£6,800) to register — at the whim of the minister — rather than the standard R10.

His task now, he says, is to make the newspaper more accessible. "We are a serious newspaper and we don't write about sex and scandals and disasters. We only write about political, social and economic issues. South African newspaper readers are very lazy: a Times or a Guardian or an Independent could never really survive in Afrikaans. In fact this newspaper is the highest quality newspaper ever to survive in Afrikaans.

"But the important thing is not only to shake up the Afrikaans press but the language as well. Afrikaners never translated words like 'power sharing' or 'congress of the people' or 'freedom charter' which kept them as alien concepts. Afrikaans has always been seen as the language of the oppressor. We're playing a part in turning this round by translating these terms and saying no, it's the language of the people which has been hijacked. Afrikaans can also be the language of the liberator." Du Preez says he has never taken too much notice of the emergency media regulations — "if you looked at the letter of the law you would never publish a newspaper" — and therefore the change for him since February 2 is a drop in the level of harassment. He has no plans — nor resources — to turn his paper into a daily. "We are in perpetual opposition," he says. "Our style is punchy, virile journalism. Subtlety is not our speciality."

ONE small sign that the South African Broadcasting Corporation is inching towards establishing a reputation for more impartial news coverage was the dropping, in March, of the nightly editorial comment from its main television service. The official reason for the end of this discredited slot — government propoganda at its crudest — was that "such talks are no longer suitable". Since February 2, even its fiercest critics have admitted that the SABC is trying to cover a fuller spectrum of political debate.

The corporation itself would say that change came earlier than February. "It was the middle of last year that we started on a new approach," says Carel van der Merwe, the Afrikaner director of news who rejoined the news division 18 months ago, before the last election.

"We had done a lot of research, looking at social and political findings. And, at the end, we sat down and decided there were 240 statements of fact about the trends we found in South African society. Then we set ourselves four tasks. And we started negotiation with 14 political parties and 16 leaders. By the end of our discussions we had identified 23 national issues. Then we said let's have election debates in five different formats." This is typical SABC-speak — desperately bureaucratic, determined to confound you with statistics to demonstrate the complexity of South African politics, and convince you of the hard task the corporation has in reflecting it. Journalists in the SABC had inhibited themselves in the past, he agrees. "But I don't want to delve into the time before I came back to news. We have a new situation, new trends in this country, and a new news service that reflects it.

"I accept that one of our critical risk factors was that we were looked upon as the lackey of the government. We can't deny that. But I believe we are already undergoing a complete turnaround in the image of the SABC as a reporter of news."

But although reporting of the ANC and other unbanned organisations is now a nightly occurrence, the changes at the SABC are still, ultimately, a reflection of the agenda set by the government under a state president who does not interfere with the broadcast media to the extent his predecessor did. Because the government no longer refers to Nelson Mandela as a terrorist, neither does the SABC. The SABC's view of the changing political scene is a mirror of that urged on the country by the government.

Mr van der Merwe protests that politics must be handled delicately by the corportion. "For us as journalists it is easy to switch, but for the South African public . . . suddenly they have to accept that people they were told were former terrorists are political leaders, and they must accept black faces on a white screen."

What the SABC believes, he says, is that there should be "purposeful reporting and support for the currents of patterns of moderation in our society."

There is, he says, a "common set of values" which the SABC must reflect. What are these? "Free enterprise is one. Streams of moderation another. Intensification of community values, a third." He says that the SABC cannot suddenly just assume that, because politics is changing, everything will change. "We have to report on government processes and government departments as they still are. We have to report on what is going on in the so-called homelands even though these structures are under attack from various political groups in a hurry for change."

Reporting on the negotiations towards change means reflecting all shades of opinion, he says, which means not assuming that the ANC has a monopoly on black support. Support for "moderate opinion" would seem to include Chief Buthelezi's Inkatha but exclude the radicals in the ANC, the Pan Africanist Congress, and parties to the right of the National Party (which also complain they find it difficult to get spokesmen on the SABC).

The SABC was set up in 1936, a supposed independent service with a charter along BBC lines. From its vast complex on a hill overlooking Johannesburg, where the security is formidable, it runs 23 radio services in Afrikaans, English, and nine African languages; and four television channels in seven languages. The first of these, TV1, started in 1976. TV1 is the flagship, with programmes in Afrikaans and English. TV2 and TV3 are black-language channels. TV4, started in 1985, is described as multi-cultural entertainment and sports, mainly in English and Afrikaans.

SABC also runs the external radio services for the government, but recently axed its European broadcasts leading to speculation about the service as a whole.

SABC has a monopoly on television and, therefore, on television news. This may change under pressure from the four newspaper groups, which have a stake in M-NET, a subscription channel. The government is considering their request to run a news service.

Other things, too, may change: last month the government set up a task force to conduct a "full investigation" into broadcasting, including consideration of whether it should be privatised. This has created some controversy, partly over the lack of commercial sector representation , in particular of groups lobbying for radio and television to be opened to independent outsiders. The task force has also been seen as a move to pre-empt a black government.

The SABC news division is integrated in the sense that it serves both radio and television, but there are separate news rooms for the different languages.

The news agendas for the white and black channels tend to be very different.Christo Kritzinger, editor-in-chief of television news, says this is a matter for the news editors themselves. It is a bewilderingly complicated operation. The night I was there, the TV1 newsroom (60 per cent Afrikaners, 40 per cent English) was leading its 8pm news bulletin on the debate about nationalisation and the ANC — first, a report from parliament; second, a speech from Mandela in which he had significantly softened his position. The Afrikaans news earlier that evening had led on the Harms Commission in London. The two white languages take it in turns through the week to present the main hour-long news programme.

On TV2 (Zulu and Xhosa), 80 per cent of whose audience lives in Natal, the lead was soldiers going into the Natal trouble spots. On TV3 (north and south Sotho and Tswana), the first three stories were about the "independent homelands". Both black channels had Mandela's speech as the fifth item.

The language and regional differences of the television services divide them but this, in the end, means race. TV1 tends to have white presenters, TV2 and 3 black. TV2 and 3 have black game shows and entertainment. All the top jobs are in white hands.

The same division occurs in advertising, although this is changing. Quentin Green, the deputy director general responsible for finance and administration, mentioned that he had just been asked to approve an advertisement for TV1 with a "heavily black accented" English voice over. "Does one go for language purity in advertisements or accept that there are different accents in this country?" he mused. "TV1 is the English language channel and people like the English to be pure. A year ago we might have refused it. Now we are trying to move away from being pedantic about these issues. Blacks are also resistance to the correct accent in their languages you know." He hinted that he had let this particular commercial go ahead partly because he believed the advertising agency had expected it to be refused. "But we have to be careful advertisers are not playing a political role to test the SABC."

Advertising is important to the SABC — R500 million (£114 million) a year, compared with R150 million in licence fees. Over at the programme division, Theuns van Heerden, deputy director-general responsible for programmes, spends the highest proportion of his television budget on TV1. He says this is because the black channels have a smaller audience, as ownership of television sets is lower among blacks than among whites.

About a third of the budget is spent on programmes from overseas: not British drama, because there is an Equity boycott, but a good deal from America. Murder She Wrote is the most popular programme, but there's also LA Law, thirtysomething, Dynasty, Golden Girls and numerous others, including Die Waltons in Afrikaans.

The sensitivity about race had that week penetrated Van Heerden's drama department. "TV Star Fanny WAS coloured" The Star had run on its front page, the latest development in a fierce debate about Barney Barnato, the SABC's main home-grown drama. The row was over whether Barnato, a 19th century gold and diamond millionaire, had a white wife, as his descendants insist, or whether Fanny Bees was classified Coloured, as SABC had portrayed her. The Star had come to the SABC's aid by revealing that records in the Bureau for Genealogy at the Human Sciences Research Council showed Fanny was "a non-white person born in the Cape".

Van Heerden was enjoying the sensation of being on the "right" side of the debate. "We didn't even think about showing her as Coloured. These are the facts. Otherwise people would have accused the SABC of doing something funny."

He says the corporation is slowly beginning to redefine its programme policy, which means more effort to mix black and white actors and music, for instance. "Eventually we just have to look after the minorities, and there are some in each language group." He looks a bit nervous. "If you say things are changing too loudly, people will think you're advocating this or that. Already there are people who accuse the SABC of being part and parcel of the ANC."

15 Voices on the line

Georgina Henry

JOHN ROBBIE picks up the phone. *"You do not have the right* to tell us your opinions. You are an immigrant in this country, you are Irish and *you must not* tell us what should be in this country," said the voice, quivering with anger, swearing blue down the line.

When Robbie gets a word in he says: "You're not listening to what I am saying, you stupid woman. The majority of people in this country don't have the right to vote. Are you saying we don't have a right to voice an opinion either?"

The exchange is being broadcast live on radio. Robbie is the host of a late night phone-in on Radio 702, a two-hour programme, which is so unusual in South African broadcasting that people in Johannesburg constantly tell you to listen in. Robbie gets some abusive calls, but many who ring up propounding views from across the political and racial spectrum also thank him for being there. He doesn't hide his views, but they like him all the same. Robbie, who has been doing the job for a few months, presides over the most open political show on the air. 702, as a station which gets its licence from Bophuthatswana, is seen by its audience as an independent voice, a world away from the radio services run by the South African Broadcasting Corporation.

Every Monday, for example, Robbie's Talk at Ten becomes State of the Nation. Monday April 23 was a typical agenda: talks about talks due to start the following week between the Government and the ANC, right wing vigilantes arming, and the continuing violence in Natal. At the weekend, a 9-year-old girl had been necklaced. "It looks like one hell of a mess," observed Robbie. "Sometimes you might think South Africans live in totally different worlds. But isn't that the point? Are races here basically different or have they been forced by law into these different worlds? Think about it. Call me and give me your views."

Robbie's show has earned a special place in South African radio because it is just about the only live forum where black and white, Afrikaner and English speakers, right and left exchange views. Part of his credibility with the white right stems from his background. A former Irish (south of Dublin) rugby player, who not only broke the international boycott and played in South Africa but chose to settle here, he doubles up as 702's sports editor. He's a sympathetic ear to the Afrikaner. His credibility with blacks is that, while he lets the right have their say, he forces callers to defend their views and he puts the other side. Similarly, he tackles black callers for their views on whites, violence and the ANC. Listening in, you realise how delicately he has to tread to keep the show open to the range of views that is its strength. On this particular night, white caller after caller wanted to talk about the ANC.

Alan: "Since Nelson Mandela was released he's been running around all the time overseas and in the meantime his own people are busy killing each other. He's not worried."

Robbie: "But surely the majority of blacks are peace-loving people?"

Alan: "I wouldn't say that. While Mandela's at pop concerts there's a war going on. Black people are burning each other. The ANC is running round with illegal weapons, throwing bombs round South Africa. Something's wrong."

Robbie: "But there's an awful lot that's been wrong. Surely you must expect an upheaval when the country starts to right the wrongs?"

The next caller is an Afrikaner former rugby player. "Well John, I grew up as a Boer. When I was young, people said to me that the black man is called a certain name. I've changed as an Afrikaner and I think anyone can change. But that means the black man has to stop blaming us as well."

Another John agrees: "We have to go through a change of attitude and understand what the other side wants. But what is a black man's understanding of freedom and equal rights?"

On the phone is the first black caller of the night. "I say check the history of the ANC. It was the government that forced it to take up arms . . . Only if the white society realises we are all human beings, until such time as they accept that blacks are equal to whites and we're on the same level and with the same feelings. White people tend to decide for the black man what is right and wrong for him. We've got the same brains as white men you know."

Joe, also black, says: "I don't think there should be any doubt in the minds of whites of the hurt and destruction they have caused blacks over the years. They've been fed a lot of propaganda concerning organisations like the ANC."

Robbie: "But now we seem to be moving towards negotiation and yet Mandela is saying keep up the armed struggle. Would it not help to give it up?"

Robbie estimates that about 40 per cent of the callers to his show are black. He doesn't ask, it's a calculation based on the names which his producer in the box next door feeds him.

Later in the week, the issue of the day is police pay, since 702's lead news story has been mass resignations from the police force. Mostly it has to do with lousy pay and scorn at the increases just announced in parliament but, asks Robbie, what do people think about the statement that the police must not belong to political parties?

For the first hour, caller after caller is white and either a cop, an ex-cop, or a cop's wife, sister, mother complaining. Except for a town councillor from Boksburg, Conservative Party heartland, who's a regular caller: "They're leaving because they're not willing to work under a minister of law and order that's too spineless to defend his own people. He would rather talk to an ANC terrorist just out of jail than his own people." Robbie is careful to agree that the police have a difficult job to do but he's also trying to move the debate on to police behaviour. On the phone is an ex-cop: "Police have a rough deal. One of the most terrifying things is to be facing a mob and you know that you're under attack . . ." Robbie: "To play devil's advocate . . . what about the feelings of the crowd facing the police?"

By the end of the first hour, Robbie's concerned that all the calls are a bit "samey", for which read white. But within minutes of the show returning after the news a caller is on the line demanding to know why black people haven't been phoning. The black calls flood in after that, accusing the police of being too politically involved with the Conservatives, of racism, of intimidating Sowetans.

The debate heats up. On the line is a regular view, the "North of the Limpopo Caller", Robbie calls them. This time it's Gavin: "South Africans are lucky that they have a police force that actually works for them. Look at other countries in Africa, and see what happened when the blacks took over."

Robbie never gives his callers short shrift, but he tackles them hard when they're defending apartheid or racism. "It's when people are trying to defend the indefensible and they find they're losing the argument that they tend to get abusive," he explains as he emerges, all sweated up, after the show. "That's when they start calling me an Irish bastard who doesn't know anything." When they do, he fights back. "Andre, you're a CHICKEN!," he shouts cheerfully as Andre puts the phone down without waiting to tell Robbie why he shouldn't say the things he does. "Look, I don't want this to become a dial-a-protest show," says Robbie. "Some people see me as a raving Marxist and I get my share of death threats. But I think the show does challenge attitudes, the view that the stereotyped Afrikaner says this, the black radical that and the English liberal the other."

16 In black and white

Nomavenda Mathiane

JOURNALISTS in South Africa are experiencing grave problems. For black journalists the situation is even worse. We stand between the "system" and the "people", while at the same time facing our "masters" who are white and have no idea of the black world.

Some editors accuse black journalists of using the paper to advance their political agendas while seeing nothing wrong with a white journalist arguing a black line in the same pages.

White journalists, living in white areas, enjoy immunity. They can write any story and will never be petrol-bombed or necklaced. A white journalist can be critical of both black and white politicians. Black journalists dare not.

White journalists operate within a fairly literate society which understands media regulations, whereas the majority of black readers do not understand emergency restrictions. For them it is simple. An incident occurs in a black township and they see a black journalist. In the paper the next day no mention is made of what happened. Either the journalists are suppressing news, or they are too lazy to do their work. How are they to know that before we can publish sensitive reports we have to get police clearance?

Then comes censorship from the liberation movements. There was a time when the press had one enemy and that was the law. Falling foul of this meant detention or whatever the system deemed fit. Today we would rather face a hostile government than cross paths with the movements.

If a journalist contravenes some silly law, the worst that can happen is that he is thrown into jail and the legal process takes its course. But if a black journalist writes a story interpreted as against the movement, then anything from ostracisation, or the gutting of the journalist's house to necklacing is possible. The reporter is labelled and carries that tag for as long as the movement wants.

And yet white journalists are not treated in this way. They can ask activists sensitive questions which we would never dream of asking.

Liberation movements expect black journalists to be revolutionaries like them. We must not question, only report incidents "as they are". Our political affiliations are questioned and we are expected to toe a particular populist ideology. Putting issues into perspective may earn a black journalist a bad name.

It is difficult to sacrifice the truth for the struggle. After all, we are journalists trained to search for truth, to follow hunches, to mirror society. We also owe it to the public to inform, interpret and alert. How can we perform, when we must forever look over our shoulders? At times I wonder if the suppression of news is not an African disease. Look at the number of African journalists who are working in foreign lands simply because they dared question actions of their governments at home. African prisons are bursting at the seams with people who dared criticise the government. Do such stories reach the newspapers? If they do, are the editors brave enough to publish them? We know more about what happens in Lithuania, than about what goes on across our borders. Already the buzz-word here is about a new and changing South Africa called PASA (Post Apartheid South Africa), as though the day apartheid goes, love, goodwill, tolerance and openness will suddenly emerge. But the communities are doing nothing to clear the way for a stable and secure PASA.

Instead they are doing everything in their power to suppress any voice cautioning the erosion of human rights. It is seen as right to expose the atrocities of the system and condone those done in the name of the struggle. Black journalists are doing good work if they expose the Afrikaner farmers who exploit black workers, but become bad guys when they write about black traders in Soweto working fellow blacks as slaves in their shops.

For all the harassment and bullying of journalists, I still have faith that we will have the last laugh. I strongly believe in the African idiom that nothing lasts forever. One day Africa will learn to take criticism. In the meantime, we will continue to chronicle history as best as we can.

17 Wish you weren't there

Frank Keating's open letter to Mike Gatting

MY DEAR GATT, We know you won't come home (voluntarily, that is), but oh how we wish you would. It is as sad for us as it must be shaming for you to be defiantly and so pathetically ending your illustrious international career behind barbed wire and to the sighs of the civilised world. I was in Paris at the weekend for the rugby. The French, as you know, don't even know about French cricket. But they know all about you. Every TV news bulletin carried dramatic shots of people and children being truncheoned and tear-gassed because of your benighted trip. The tour of Gatting's pique. We all know you had been shoddily treated by the feudal mandarins of Lord's this last 18 months, but this is a vengeance with knobkerries on. When the township beatings are shown on the news, does Elaine let Andrew and James stay up to hear Daddy once so chipper and cheerful and downright inspiring put on his new face of dumb insolence and say "What happens in the townships is nothing to do with me"?

I still cannot believe it's you. We go back a long way. Remember at Montserrat against the Leeward Islands 10 years ago, when we had a party at John Woodcock's rented bungalow? A discussion about the awfulness of South Africa became pretty heated and, when Emburey and Boycott led the gang to throw me into the swimming pool, you who had just made successive scores of 2, 0, 0 and were feeling terribly low still came to my rescue. You were feeling downcast again a year later when you had lost your Test place once more in India, and rumours were flying around about an upcoming pirate tour to South Africa. Count me out, you said, playing for England was the only thing. When Emburey, captain-elect of Middlesex, was banned, you stepped up as county leader. If you hadn't, you might never have captained England in the first place and all your subsequent turbulence would never have happened and you'd have been back in the Caribbean today. You weren't even picked for the Australian tour the following winter.

I took you and Elaine, remember, to the Sportswriters' dinner-dance at the Cafe Royal. On the top table with us was the Sportsman of the Year, Daley Thompson. Could you look Daley in the eye if you met him again? How, come to that and even nearer home, could you have stomached hearing the racist jeers at Southampton in the NatWest semi last summer at your black county colleague, Norman Cowans, who had just publicly declared against your tour? "I would never take South African blood money," said Cowans. "It is an evil regime." Or didn't the reasoning and brave public repentance of another black friend of yours at Middlesex, Roland Butcher, mean a row of beans to you when he pulled out of your tour when he realised its full implications to his Christian faith and his example to his children? I could go on.

One of the glories of the English county cricket circuit is its happy multi-racialism. You are slapping that in the face with every run you make and pound you pocket. And where, even, has your firm leadership gone? Of the many stories that have filtered back home this last couple of weeks, the most grotesquely insensitive was that of the Yorkshireman, Jarvis, making sure he was first off the bus at Bloemfontein with his video-camera so he could film the demonstration of Africans that greeted you. There wasn't a full complement, because many had been beaten up on their way to seeing you. But they still make for some smashing home movies, eh? And on your arrival at Johannesburg with the blood still being mopped up at the airport I'm told the opening bat, Broad, gets a security cop to escort him furtively round the hotel grounds so he can get a few tourist shots with his camera of another demonstration that was pleading with you to get back home. Yet your party line remains "Township violence is nothing to do with us".

How quickly you have absorbed the perennially blinkered attitude of your white hosts. Can't you get up and say, "Hey, we've been misled; if the police continue with their mayhem, we're pulling out of the tour"? Or say, "Hang on, we were guaranteed the chance to foster with coaching the township cricket programme: what's happened to that"?

The truth is, for all Dr Bacher's con-trick speeches to the Wisden dinner and after, the townships don't want you near them and already, solely because of your presence, two of the famous township programmes, at Bloemfontein and Pretoria, have been disbanded. How's that for the pathetic letter to The Times from Peter May and others which saw you off, insisting your tour would "help promote the long-term cricket interests of young black enthusiasts"? If you really believed, as you and friend Graveney (what's happened to his alleged silky diplomacy, by the way?) kept repeating before you left, that you were intent "not on fat cheques but to help break down apartheid", then you have been grossly duped. Laughably, tragically so.

Your presence, after all the putrid flannel, is starkly seen to serve no purpose whatsoever except to give a game of sorts to 11 South Africans. Not forgetting the lolly, of course.

Anyway, Gatt m'dear, enjoy the rest of your stay. And the cricket, such as it is. And if anyone dies, do think again about coming back home. I know you will. All ye best, Frank

18 Wealth, the front line

Alex Brummer

IT WAS mid-morning at the dowdy Park Lane Hotel in the integrated and infectiously vibrant Hillbrow neighbourhood of Johannesburg. For the last couple of hours, a succession of young black trade union leaders, their hair glistening, their chests proclaiming the black, green and yellow emblems of the African National Congress and keeping what is disparagingly called African time, had been gathering to take part in a debate about a new political order.

Alec Erwin, economic guru of the Congress of South African Trade Unions (Cosatu), posed a central question which, in any other country since the East European free market revolutions, would have seemed obviously outmoded. Should a black government adopt the "command economic model" as pioneered in a post-revolutionary Soviet Union? Or should it follow the Scandinavian social democratic blueprint with the goal of displacing a "low wage, high cost" economy with a "low cost, high wage" economy?

Although, to the sceptical outsider, both these

models have to a degree been discredited, they are as useful a tool as any for discussing a political economy which has perverted morality and equity in a manner without parallel anywhere on the globe.

In Hillbrow, where Cosatu was in session, one might easily be deceived into thinking apartheid already has untwined. It is a "grey" neighbourhood where blacks, whites and Coloureds trade, intermingle and carouse with ease. A recently posted sales notice outside an apartment block states that, in keeping with new regulations, ownership is open to all races. Or is it?

Apartheid cannot simply be brushed aside as a political aberration — a minority taking racism to the extreme. It was an economic tool which enabled white South Africans to transform a primary economy, based on subsistence agriculture, exceptionally rich mineral deposits and an abundance of cheap and unskilled labour into a First World style economy with an efficient, modern infrastructure.

But even as economic apartheid has broken down, in response to the forces of a sophisticated capital market and a diversifying manufacturing sector, the distribution of income has remained skewed hopelessly. Thus, to many blacks, an apartment in Hillbrow remains as inaccessible as ever, because of disqualification by income and lack of mortgage finance. The abolition of the 1950 Group Areas Act, which severely curtailed property rights, will not suffice alone.

Distribution of capital, wealth and land is at the core of the economic debate about the new South Africa. Consider some basic facts: six mining finance houses led by Harry Oppenheimer's reform-minded

Anglo-American Corporation control 80 per cent of the shares quoted on the Johannesburg Stock Exchange (JSE); government-run "parastatals" (nationalised industries) are responsible for creating some 29 per cent of gross domestic product and account for as much as 40 per cent of white employment; 5 per cent of the population own 88 per cent of the wealth; more than half of all households have incomes below the recognised "poverty line". It is disparities, thrown into relief by statistics such as these, which explain the anger and illustrate the desire for root and branch economic reforms of the kind being discussed by Cosatu and the ANC, of which the former is a peculiarly powerful constituent.

But wholesale economic reform which seeks to redress past grievances, of whatever shape, does not take place in a vacuum. It is being forced by pressure from two sources: militant trade union activity aimed at redressing long-standing grievances over income, working practices and ownership patterns, and financial sanctions which have starved Africa's most successful economy of capital — the lifeline of growth. As the economic adviser to the Reserve Bank (South Africa's central bank), Dr S J Kleu, noted in an interview in his marbled 31st-floor office in Pretoria: "Financial sanctions hurt us more (than economic sanctions). They raised political consciousness about apartheid."

As a result, Dr Kleu argued: "We have a capital shortage." It is this shortage which has forced the Republic to export capital by running a current account surplus, crushed growth and contributed to an inflation rate which has veered close to 20 per cent. By the standards of deprivation and hunger in sub-Saharan Africa, the South African economy can be considered more than robust. By its own standards of wealth creation, it is a basket case.

It is on these weak pillars that a new government in Pretoria, with significant black representation, will have to build its new order. There will be some immediate benefits: any political settlement which moves the white laager toward majority rule will have an enormous impact internationally, dwarfing the euphoric response to Nelson Mandela's freedom.

It could unlock funds from the International Monetary Fund and World Bank, providing an offical imprimatur for commercial bank credits. A declared end to the "armed struggle" would mean that the gentle downward slope in defence and security spending (signalled by Finance Minister Barend du Plessis in his 1990 budget) could be steepened, provided sectarian/tribal jockeying for position — like that in the killing fields of Natal — is halted. The dismantling of the enormous apartheid-enforcing duplicate bureaucracies could release finance for black education, training and housing.

None of this can happen unless there is confidence in the future. The international markets will have to be convinced that capital will not be pitched into a political abyss. And there has to be confidence in the National government that reforms can be carried through without provoking military responses by black radicals or Afrikaner extremists. Mr Mandela's careless nationalisation talk demonstrated graphically how quickly financial optimism can vanish.

In the weeks following President F W de Klerk's historic February 2 address announcing sweeping apartheid reforms, shares in Johannesburg soared and the discount on the financial Rand, the pool of investment funds available to foreign investors, dropped to 20 per cent. Mr Mandela's nationalisation threat (already being modified) and the talk by Cosatu and others of a command economy have sent the discount back to 40 per cent, reflecting historical worries about prospects. At a time when economic thinking among the communities is moving in opposite directions — the whites towards privatisation of parastatals, the blacks towards nationalisation or dismemberment of the colossus of the mining houses — ownership patterns will shape perceptions of the new South Africa and could remove market uncertainties.

As Afrikaner stockbroker and economist, Louis C Geldenhuys, of the firm, George Huysamer & Partners, observed: "South Africa is not like a Mozambique which is in the development stage of its economic system."

Shuffling assets between the public and private sectors may help ease the respective sense of insecurity and grievance between the black and white communities, but will do nothing for economic efficiency or market confidence. A much more encouraging path would be to use American style affirmative action to accelerate black stakeholding in existing business and for governments to provide resources to build upon a flourishing culture of black enterprise. Street hawkers, black taxi syndicates and black-controlled public companies, such as Lebowa Bakeries, have demonstrated that African instincts for trade and entrepreneurship are sound.

The instruments for creating a black enterprise culture are in place: but they need huge infusions of capital to flourish effectively. Redistribution from white to black, by means of mandated ownership of the means of production, may settle some old scores. But it cannot deliver instant prosperity to the many and usher in a new era of growth throughout southern Africa.

"The National Party enter the negotiations over South Africa's future controlling the police, the army and the system of justice," argues Lawrence B Mavundra, a former black activist with the National Union of Miners, now organising small African owned businesses.

"All the ANC takes to the talks is sanctions, strikes and the rhetoric of the armed struggle." In this unequal tussle, argue the advocates of majority black rule, removing sanctions now would deprive Mr Mandela of his strongest bargaining chip.

As a tool forcing political change, economic sanctions often have been disparaged and are certainly not favoured by diplomats. Indeed, studies show that over the sweep of this century they have failed to meet their objective in a clear majority of cases. South Africa belies this experience. The imposition of sanctions, particularly the embargo on capital, undermined the fabric of prosperity on which the wealth of the white laager was built. Growth has given way to stagnation; price stability to rampant inflation; a strong labour market has given way to large scale unemployment and social unrest; investment has been halted and the legendary white standard of living has come under enormous stress. There is capital famine that threatens not just the wealth creation of the present but confidence in the future.

Critics of sanctions, from Mrs Thatcher holding forth in the Commons to an enlightened construction engineer holding forth at a Johannesburg dinner party, point out that a side effect of sanctions has been widespread rationalisation in South African mining and industry. This has cost blacks their jobs and condemned them to squalor in the tin shanty towns which now ring the large conurbations. But understandably, after four decades of large scale economic inequalities, blacks have no reason to believe that, if sanctions were to be lifted the new wealth and investment would be shared any more equally than in the past — unless there is black government to protect their interests.

The best measure of the effectiveness of sanctions is the consensus, on all sides of the political and business spectrum, that they are working. Leading officials of Cosatu argue that financial sanctions have been a most effective tool leading to deep seated structual changes in the economy. At the Reserve Bank Dr Kleu notes that simply to meet its debt commitments South Africa needed a surplus of R6 billion (£1.36 billion) a year. "That is a considerable sum for a country such as South Africa to meet ... it is a restraint on growth," he added.

The heads of such national institutions as the Small Business Development Corporation, with the goal of bringing money to black enterprise, say that the capital famine means they cannot fulfil the demand for credit. While Tom Main, the chief executive of the Chamber of Mines, which represents the large mining houses, explains that financial sanctions have played havoc with the economics of the goldmines which in 1988 still accounted for 13 per cent of gross domestic product. Because the National Government needs to maintain a low exchange rate — to finance exports so as to meet debt repayments — the rand price for gold had not fully reflected increases in dollar price for bullion, at a time when labour and other extraction costs have been soaring.

The president of the JSE, Tony Norton, agrees that the "biggest sanction was debt repayment." He notes that the Financial Rand (used for investment) climbed briefly after Mr De Klerk's February speech in the belief that sanctions might be lifted. However, for the moment, financial sanctions remain in place, although the immediate danger was relieved by the 1987 debt rescheduling package.

This has not been enough, however, to forestall crisis in each of South Africa's economies: the first world economy of the white business community; the second world economy of the Afrikaans dominated bureaucracy and the third world economy of the townships and subsistence homelands. During the 1970s and the early 1980s South Africa maintained a healthy growth rate of 5-6 per cent annually. But with the uprisings in the townships, repression by the National Party and sanctions, the country plunged into deep recession in 1985 — it has still to fully recover. Growth in 1989 was a paltry 2.1 per cent with the economy tailing off sharply in the final quarter by 1.5 per cent.

The government is paying the price for past profligacy including an undisciplined fiscal policy and loose monetary policy, embedded in the notion that there were no bounds to the heights of the gold price. The result has been an inflation explosion with prices currently rising in the mid-teens. The new governor of the Reserve Bank, Chris Stals, has pushed the discount rate to 17 per cent and the banks are being forced to cut back on lending through increased reserve requirements. The result is a squeeze on investment by white business weakening the nation's economic architecture.

Nowhere is this squeeze being felt more sharply that in the Afrikaner dominated public sector, where the nationalised industries are being prepared for privatisation. While the factors behind this drive for an enterprise economy are complex, the effect of privatisation is to ease budgetary pressures. Although South Africa may have the best roads and telephones in Africa, its public services — from education to hospitals — are in lamentable shape. Even the Groote Schuur Hospital in Cape Town, where Dr Christiaan Barnard carried out his pioneering heart transplant surgery, is in financial difficulty and has been forced into a public appeal to save its famed heart unit.

The brunt of the sanctions burden, however, has fallen on South Africa's third world — the unskilled black labourer. According to official statistics unemployment stands at just 10.7 per cent. But the data, like so much else in South Africa, is corrupted. Because the homelands are not technically part of the Republic and the residents in the sprawling shanty towns are technically non-persons in the forbidden place, they are not counted. Thus the best guesses suggest real unemployment in the range 25-30 per cent.

Sanctions, economic and financial, have worked and are keeping the pressure on. But at a crushing human price.

JUST A BLOCK from the the ultimate symbol of white wealth in South Africa, the brick and glass tower of the Johannesburg Stock Exchange, it is now possible to smell, hear and feel the atmosphere of Africa. Jeppe Street, immediately north of the central business district with its thrusting skyscrapers, is arrayed with stall holders selling fragrant spices, sweetcorn scorching in aromatic braziers, carrier bags decorated with the New York Statue of Liberty and fresh vegetables: giant tomatoes, papaya, sweet potatoes and greens piled high on groaning cardboard boxes. High pitched Zulu and Xhosa voices, and brightly costumed African women balancing baskets, delicately tread a path among the hawkers and the honking ranks of mini-van cabs.

The rise of what the South Africans call the "informal sector" of the economy is perhaps the most encouraging evidence of pace of change in a system where black business enterprise was generally illicit outside the townships. Much of the activity of black business might be seen by radicals as tainted, since it has depended on white patronage, as in the case of the 250 black shoe-shiners provided with equipment. Cleaning the shoes of affluent white financiers outside the JSE must be regarded as humbling, if not humiliating. But like other black enterprises it demonstrates the underdeveloped trading, entrepreneurial and artisan skills which, given proper opportunity — through training, affirmative action and finance — could blossom.

The street hawkers with their trinkets, shoes and fruit are at the base of a business pyramid. Immediately above them are black taxi associations which have taken advantage of the breakdown of apartheid in transport to set up fleets and syndicates of taxis which service all sections on the community and have largely displaced the despised government controlled

South African Transport System (SATS) — associated by the African with the miserable forced commutes from the homelands. Although many of the taxi syndicates are controlled by whites, the system is largely operated by blacks who share in the proceeds.

Next on the black enterprise hierarchy are small and medium sized companies financed and advised by Afrikaner bureaucracies such as the Small Business Development Corporation (SBDC) and the Development Bank of South Africa. This, despite its National Party heritage and management structure, is financing an increasing number of infrastructure projects in the townships and homelands. More importantly it stands ready to help finance land reform.

At the apex of the pyramid there are now a handful of larger black businesses. Most prominently there is the empire controlled by R J P Maponya, which ranges from township supermarkets to banks, and includes a string of racehorses. There are now at least two publicly quoted black managed and controlled companies quoted on the stock exchange including Lebowa Bakeries, based in the homelands, with outlets in the large cities, including Johannesburg.

What is something of a mystery is the contribution which the smaller black businesses, the informal sector, make to the economy. Dr Ben Vosloo of the SBDC estimates that there are one million businesses in the informal sector accounting for 8 per cent of the gross domestic product. Some estimates are even higher, suggesting the informal economy accounts for as much as 15-20 per cent. Whatever the size, it will remain limited in its scope and growth without abolition of apartheid and access to capital.

Mr Vosloo argues that the financial limits imposed on his organisation by the capital famine (partly the result of sanctions) is "totally foolish and suicidal." He notes bitterly that West Germany already has promised some 3.5 billion Deutschmarks to the East but there has been no similar scale commitment by the National Party government and SBDC's private sector shareholders to advancing the black economy. Nevertheless, on a mini-scale the SBDC has not been without its success.

Its showcase development at Pennyville, on the outskirts of Soweto, provides an illustration of how black business can work, providing it receives subcontracts from the white controlled mining houses and finance from government institutions. The enterprises are located in a converted factory, broken down into an "industrial park" of small businesses. Paradoxically, at least two of the African companies visited were in the security business: one making locks and another fabricating iron fences. Thus white money is being used to back African firms making devices designed to shield wealthy whites from marauding young blacks resentful of the wealth distribution.

Isaac Mdalose, 38, a skilled silk screen printer who spent three years unemployed was finally able to use his training when the SBDC agreed to fund him and Anglo-American agreed to buy his product. As a sideline Mr Mdalose, whose turnover has now reached R30,000 to R40,000 a month offers a souvenir: an ANC car sticker embossed with the bold insignia. Despite his support for the ANC's political struggle he is keen to distance himself from disputed proposals to nationalise the mining giants which are among his clients.

An important pre-condition to black economic development is an improvement in the infrastructure in the areas where most blacks have been forced to live: the townships and the homelands. The African Development Bank (ADB), which is lending R800 million a year is seeking to pump funds into black cities and rural townships and has adopted the American practice of dealing with local black leaders and contractors. It argues that even if the homelands are scrapped, as is expected, as a result of political negotiations, development funds will still be needed.

What will be most important in the view of ADB chief executive Dr Simon Brand, is that the government does not give in to the pressure from the right and backs land reform with "affirmative action." This would entail breaking down vast land holdings into smaller plots and setting up financial mechanisms to allow blacks to buy-in. Without such steps there can be no serious redistribution of wealth.

Such forward thinking, in institutions founded and run by Afrikaners, is a measure of the improving attitudes towards black capability and enterprise.

TOWNSHIP FEVER, the thundering protest musical playing at the Market Theatre in Johannesburg, provides insight as to why ownership structures for business are so passionately discussed as South Africa contemplates its new economic order. The script is built around a gruesomely violent 1987 strike of black workers against SATS, the sprawling state owned corporation, which for much of this century has been a cornerstone of apartheid. SATS represented all that was evil: it segregated passengers by race; it moved workers hundreds of kilometres from the homelands to the cities in appalling conditions; its work gangs were confined to male hostels without conjugal visits and its prestige airline offshoot — SAA — was blocked to black advancement. Now that South Africa is moving towards majority rule, which would give blacks a measure of control over an Afrikaner-run institution, the National Party government, and SATS itself, is preparing for privatisation as part of Mr De Klerk's drive to maintain a free enterprise economy. His government, taking a lead from Mrs Thatcher, has already privatised ISCOR — the publicly controlled Iron and Steel Corporation — raising R6 billion. The government hopes to bring a series of other "parastatals" to the market. These include SATS (or at least its airline offshoot SAA); Eskom, the electricity generating giant which could raise R55 billion; Post & Telecommunications; and ABAKOR, the South African Abattoir Corporation.

The timing of the privatisation drive could not be worse. It comes as the more radical forces inside the ANC, notably the black trade unions, are pushing hard in the opposite direction. Far from allowing the parastatals to fall into private hands, the ANC would like to widen public ownership. Nationalisation is a key element of the Mandela rhetoric, although the ardour has cooled in recent public statements, as a response to the pounding he has taken in the South African business press and the down draught on the JSE. However, in much the same way that the ANC distrusts the parastatals, which have operated as a social safety net for less well-off whites, it also distrusts the mining finance houses which have grown into powerful international conglomerates with the support of a cheap black labour force. Like the parastatals, the mining houses have largely condemned

African workers to the lowliest and most arduous labouring tasks. It is against this social and labour background that Cosatu and the ANC have adopted nationalisation ideology. But it is also clear that they are looking for alternatives to simply taking Anglo-American, Rembrandt, Goldfields and the other mining houses directly under state control. In a paper on post-apartheid economics Vella Pillay, a personal economic adviser to Mr Mandela, explored some alternatives such as the possibility of taking state control of two large investment institutions — Old Mutual and Sanlam — which between them would give the state a strong say in how the private sector in South Africa was run. This might enable a new post-apartheid government to earmark some proportion of funds for financial institutions which service the black economy. Unbundling could also be an option.

Amid this ferment of ideas on the best way in which a post-apartheid government might use the levers available to advance a black agenda of wealth redistribution, the rush to privatisation appears discordant. Certainly, it has deeply disturbed the black community, which has staged a series of anti-privatisation protests including an angry march on the JSE. Aside from the traditional ill-will to SATS, black passion over privatisation stems from the ISCOR experience where up to 20,000 jobs, many of them black, were rationalised to prepare the company for a quotation. Moreover, although black jobs historically have been the least well paid at the parastatals, they have been considerably better rewarded than unskilled posts in mining and manufacturing.

The unions argue that privatisation is a ruse. It is an attempt by the white minority to ensure that the parastatals are safely in white business hands, out of the range of black government, before majority rule begins. However, the government has other strong reasons for wishing to press ahead. Not least is the budget squeeze. The R6 billion generated by the ISCOR flotation eased the government's fiscal squeeze — the result of sanctions. "There is a clear financial motive," argues David Lewis, a University of Cape Town economist. Lewis also believes, however, that Mr De Klerk has caught the free market bug of the 1980s.

This is a philosophical change for the National Party which, when it came to power, was committed (like some radical ANC elements) to nationalisation and over four decades made no real effort to hand back the public sector to the markets. Mr De Klerk has now adopted the "free enterpise system" as he frequently stated during his Brian Walden interview. His government's recent budget, which sought to change priorities, offered a number of concessions to capital including the gradual elimination of the South African equivalent of stamp duty.

The JSE president, Tony Norton, is among those who believe that popularisation of shareholding is important at a time when "many private investors in South Africa have become heavy disinvestors." Flotations of public corporations help fulfil this goal, particularly if, as in the case of ISCOR, workers are offered shareholdings as part of the flotation. Similarly, Anglo-American has sought to broaden its shareholder base by offering stock options to workers.

The most encouraging aspect of the privatisation-versus-nationalisation argument is that as the ANC and the government lock each other into a political process both sides are retreating from financial extremism. Mr Mandela now says that he will only nationalise the mines, banks and other industries if it "strengthens the economy." The National Party too is stepping back amid concerns that attempts to take SATS to the market could be "very bloody," as David Lewis says. Capitalism could yet be saved by common sense.

THE YOUNG Afrikaner guide at the Doornfontein Gold Mine, less than an hour's drive through brush and slag heaps from Johannesburg, was earnestly explaining the rigorous training regimen for new mine recruits. Among the most important procedures, he assured us, was "acclimatisation", the way in which workers are prepared for the high temperatures deep underground where the richest gold reefs are located.

Do all miners go though this? one asked. "No," came the hesitant reply, "only the blacks. Why? "It is to do with pigmentation. There's research which shows that blacks absorb the heat less well than whites." It was a reply delivered in innocent ignorance. When in comes to mining, still the fount of South Africa's wealth, there is no sign, in the pits at least, that racism is dormant or apartheid dead. Many practices seem designed to inflict indignity: acclimatisation consists of herding large numbers of blacks into a hall, forcing them to strip naked in the presence of white supervisory staff while they are submitted to four hours of heat and humidity. This "training" lasts for four days.

It is symbolic of the way in which the mining finance houses, in this case Goldfields (now part of the Rembrandt group) treat their black labour as second class citizenry. At Doornfontein black labourers live in clean, modern hostels. But they are enclosed behind high steel fences topped with rolled barbed wire in compounds with the acrid smell of prisons. They are separated from their wives and families, who are as many as 800 kilometres away in the homelands. White miners live with their families in comfortable detached villas just a few kilometres from the pit.

Black "labourers" as they are officially called, perform the menial tasks of working in three-foot or so of crawl space, drilling holes to place the dynamite and removing ore and debris while the whites do the more "skilled" tasks such as operating the shafts and underground locomotives. Blacks work underground in their own flimsy clothes, whereas whites are provided with protective overalls, gloves and jackets. The apartheid regulations which prevented blacks from moving into more skilled jobs have been removed: but they have been replaced with an education qualification which is almost impossible for African workers to meet given the parlous state of black education. For the privilege of working the mines blacks are paid R500 to R600 a month, with Anglo-American paying slightly better than its compatriots within the Chamber of Mines.

The condition of the black miners, who are represented by the black National Union of Mineworkers, and their relationship with the mine-owners is central to the economic success of a post-apartheid South Africa. There are some important paradoxes in the relationship. Anglo-American, the largest house which alone controls an astonishing 43.5 per cent of the market capitalisation on the JSE, is the most politically progressive of the mining finance houses with its graduate black employment schemes, employee share options and its pioneering dialogue with the ANC opened by former chairman Gavin Relly. But its mines, the foundations of an apparently enlightened empire with interests in everything from newspapers to breweries, are anchored in mining and its oppressive labour system.

Despite all its sophistication South Africa's wealth and the importance of its capital markets are inextricably linked with mining and in particular gold. This ensures the NUM, a significant constituent of the ANC, a loud say in any political or economic settlement. The mining industry (gold, coal, diamonds, platinum and other minerals) contributes some 25.3 per cent of the gross national product; it directly employs just under 800,000 people; constitutes some 8 per cent of the government's tax base and in some regions, notably the Orange Free State, is the overarching factor in the economy. Some 65 per cent of mineral exports are represented by gold. Thus the relationship between the NUM and the Chamber of Mines, together with the free market price of bullion, are among the most important determinants of South Africa's future.

The unions and the mine owners are poles apart. Sipping tea from a bone china cup in the Chamber of Mines headquarters, the chief executive Tom Main warns that any attempt to nationalise the gold mines would drive away the capital required to develop new production and sustain the South African economy. He draws comfort for South Africa in the rejection of centrally managed economies in the Soviet Union and Eastern bloc: "I don't believe that the leaders of the black people of South Africa that are now emerging are that rigid in their thinking, or that committed to dogma, not to be able to reject outmoded principles that are now totally discredited."

A few blocks away at the NUM headquarters Martin Nichol, Head of Collective Bargaining, coolly explains why the black unions want more power over the mines in which they work and live: "There is systematic discrimination in the mines," he argued. "It is part of the inbuilt system of racial oppression." He ticks off the symbols including acclimatisation and black hostels noting that these are as important to the union's members as an increase in wages. Nevertheless, the NUM — after a succession of pay awards — is seeking a further 35 per cent in the current pay round. In an effort to improve pay and ease racist conditions the NUM has pressed industrial action most recently at the Unisel mine controlled by Gencor and at the Freegold and Vaal Reefs mines controlled by Anglo-American.

The mining houses grew rich in the fat years following 1972, when the free market price of gold soared from the $35 per ounce fixed rate to more than $800 amid a surge in inflation throughout the West. But as price pressures subsided among the market economies in the 1980s the gold price tumbled. While the bullion price briefly surged this year (it was at an average of $406 per once in the first quarter) it is now back at $380 per ounce. It would require a doomsday scenario in the American economy, brought down perhaps by an avalanche of debt, to envisage gold replacing the dollar as the world's premier store of value. The combination of rising labour costs and a static gold price have cut the profit margins for gold mines from 70 per cent in 1979 to 15 per cent now. This in an industry where reaching the reef, some 3,000 metres below ground, has become increasingly costly.

None of this justifies the inhumanity of the lingering apartheid system in the mines enforced by the Afrikaner unions with the acquiesence of the mine owners. It has to be changed and the mining finance houses have the resources to do it: that they haven't has deservedly made them international pariahs. Redistribution of resources has to begin at the pit where South Africa's legendary riches have been created.

But business, despite its debt to the black workforce, cannot carry the burden of economic reform alone. Financial sanctions have been an effective enough source of neuralgia for the government for it to recognise the necessity of political change. The first round of negotiations between the ANC and National Party are testament to this. Having brought itself some political peace, the government will soon have to focus on an economic peace.

It is plain that the economic status quo is unsustainable. Such efforts as there have been by whites to share wealth and opportunity are paltry. The most recent budget is reformist by Afrikaner standards, but does not begin to tackle the enormous gap in education and training which will be necessary if blacks are to be better prepared to move from unskilled roles up the corporate and bureaucratic hierachy. What is needed, to use an East European analogy, is a Marshall Plan for black South Africa. But like the economic reforms in Poland and Hungary they must be internally generated before receiving the backing of outsiders — the IMF, World Bank and development community. They must make accelerated affirmative action in the parastatals, the bureaucracy and the business community a condition of assistance. There must be fundamental land reform and free availiability of finance to back it up. Black trade unions must be fully recognised and integrated into the economic structure and black entrepreneurship must be fully funded and enthusiastically encouraged. The white monopoly on management skills must be broken. It can and should be done without a Marxist-style, one-party revolution — the model which has been a stunning failure elsewhere in Africa.

But Pretoria and Johannesburg — in the shape of Anglo American, Gencor, Rembrandt and the others — must realise that, if they lack the will for change, they can expect mandatory reforms and ultimately dismemberment and oblivion.

19 White woman's burden

Judy Rumbold

SHEENA DUNCAN is accustomed to finding her garden hose chopped up into convenient bite-sized servings, to discovering a brace of dead cats swinging from her doorpost, to having 250 sandwiches (assorted fillings) she didn't order delivered to her house. Duncan is a leading member of the Black Sash organisation in South Africa and refuses to yield to the relentless campaign of police harassment against her. "I think dignified silence is the best method. To object is to invite further abuse. It's like the way you have to handle Buthelezi when he attacks you — pretend you didn't notice."

Since its formation in 1955, the Black Sash has been a constant source of irritation to upholders of apartheid. Its crime was to reject the lifestyle of your average white middle-class woman — a heady whirl of golf, bridge, tennis, and an army of black maids to skivvy — in favour of mobilising against the National Party's Senate Law, devised to disfranchise Coloured voters, who were still on the Common Voters Roll.

"Right!", shrieks Beulah Rollnick from the other end of the advice office. You wouldn't want to mess with her, a textbook matron in vast floral dress. She tosses away her pen in exasperation. "I've had enough! I'm not sure I'm getting the right end of this stick!".

A black woman is sitting downwind of the outburst and nearly falls off her stackable plastic chair. Mabella's smooth, unlined features are strangers to the muscular demands of hope or happiness, and she cuts a wretched figure in nylon crocheted beret and what looks like an old Woolworths overall. There is a bunch of carrier bags in the synthetic mêlée, surely harbouring gold bullion from the way they're being cradled.

Her problem is that she's been distributing leaflets for a house renovations company, and was told by her employer that she would receive R30 (about £7) for every customer that followed it up. According to Mabella's employer, nobody came back. Mabella thinks differently. Beulah reckons the spurious verbal agreement sounds fugged and exploitative, but there is nothing she can do without proof. Mabella has none. Beulah refers Mabella to legal aid and says be there at seven in the morning or else.

It's only 8.30 on a Tuesday morning and already the waiting area is packed shoulder-to-shoulder with downtrodden blacks, fully expecting to have their problems solved with a single swipe of Beulah's magic pen across an official form. Every case is a quagmire of deceit and exploitation, she says, and navigating a route to justice is laborious.

"Forty-three per cent of the people who come into the office are unorganised workers. They usually come when they've lost their jobs to complain that they weren't given letters or unemployment cards. At this stage we take the opportunity to check whether they were being paid properly in the first place, because the exploitation of people who don't belong to unions is appalling. The majority of black workers aren't unionised. The other 67 per cent are either homeless or with problems related to housing, state pension, unemployent insurance, workman's compensation . . ." Beulah's voice trails off — weary with 10 years of legal wrangling.

There was a time when life at the advice office was more leisurely. In the beginning it was a genteel, ladylike kind of set-up, a bit of a hobby. Volunteers wore hats to work, called each other Mrs this or that, and sat gossiping with their knitting and pastel sprigged writing paper. On the rare occasion a client would come through the door, there would be flustered slapstickery while the women tripped over each other to help.

The Black Sash became a political welfare organisation by mistake, casual coffee talk about the state of the nation turning to rock solid commitment in the time it takes a Rich Tea biscuit to deconstruct. Judith Hawarden, the group's current chairwoman, remembers their changing role: "So many organisations were banned, that Black Sash had a great responsibility because we were protected by our whiteness, our middle classness and, perhaps, our gender. We weren't banned like many of the black organisations, and we didn't experience massive detentions of our members. It meant that we *had* to respond and fill the gap."

The first Black Sash advice office was set up as a bail fund to get black women who had refused to carry passes (identity documents which restricted movement) out of prison while they awaited trial so they could be with their children. Involvement with those women led to a better understanding of the persecution which the pass laws inflicted. So advice offices were gradually opened up in different cities, and it was this work that really established Black Sash's credibility.

"It took a long time for the idea of an advice office to catch on," says Sheena Duncan, "especially in the political climate after Sharpeville and the banning of the ANC. The repression and the state of emergency succeeded in crushing black resistance for a whole decade."

Now that their customers form queues round the block, knitting and chat has been replaced by bustling industry, and the closest they come to the jam 'n' doily comparisons of the past is having hat-pins plunged into their backsides when they stage one of their trademark street corner protests. These stabbing attacks often precede a barrage of water-filled condoms. Ethel Walters of the Black Sash remembers being unceremoniously pelted. "The police would arrest the attackers, take them round the corner, then let them go so they could come back and do it again."

Their public protests entail nothing more provocative than standing in mute, sisterly solidarity ("sometimes we want to shout back, but it was always our guiding principle not to respond") wearing black sashes, while carrying banners which read: Stop Detention Without Trial, Release All Detainess, or simply Stop The Violence. But their calm seems to incense their detractors even more. Sheena Duncan has seen it all. "You get some real right-wing abuse. One

WHITE WOMAN'S BURDEN

man actually drove his car up on to the pavement and tried to mow us down, and sometimes when you see them reaching across to their glove compartment, their faces distorted with hatred and anger, you wonder if they're going for a gun; they all carry them."

Beulah Rollnick reads a laboriously handwritten letter, from a man in overalls, crumpled and dirty from his wrestling with words and worry. His eyes are as luckless as a fruit machine that has never experienced even a two-cherry run.

"My problem is on the 8/3/90 at night my teeth started with a horrible pain. So, on the 9/3/90 when I must go to work, my teeth was much pain and my head was also headache. My face was very swell when I looked at my mirror. I went to my work at Golden Lay and they must also see themselves that I really sick. I work for the whole day until 5 o'clock. At the following day I was much weaker. So I did not went to work since from 10/3/90. Then my boss say I discharged. He spoke nothing about notice. He spoke nothing about my share of leave pay. He spoke nothing about the reason why I must sign off . . ."

Beulah takes time to congratulate the man for articulating his problems so eloquently, then throws down the biro. This time it disembowels on impact with the floor. There must be a whole pile of broken pens somewhere in the building.

20 Mothers of a nation

Judy Rumbold

MOTHERHOOD is a big deal in white South African society. The term "volksmoeder" — Mother of the Nation — is a coveted accolade synonymous with successful passage to kitchen sink via labour ward. Lou-Marie Kruger, one of a younger generation of progressive-thinking women, is researching a book on the cult of the volksmoeder ("She rocks the cradle, she rules the world") and finds the concept worrying. "These women are all becoming mothers of the nation rather than women of the nation. Mothers in the struggle rather than women in the struggle."

Jacqueline Kock is a writer and single by choice, but will be granted little credence as a woman in white society until she has proved herself as a sort of Katie Boyle/Mrs Thatcher hybrid, with a working set of child-bearing hips. It irritates her: "If I see another T-shirt saying 'Mother for the Struggle' I'm going to scream. I'm tempted to get one printed saying 'Childless Old Spinster for the Struggle' to see how that goes down." In a university lecture Marike de Klerk encouraged maternal empiricism by saying, "We as mothers should assert ourselves in politics because we have special qualities we can bring to it."

There is a strong tradition of powerful conservative women's organisations in South Africa. "They say they are apolitical," says Lou-Marie Kruger, "and although they are confined to a domestic environment, they have been very powerful in getting their own way indirectly: by working with their children, by becoming teachers, by forming welfare organisations. They are more guilty of Afrikaner nationalism than people tend to think."

So strong is mother love in white South Africa that feminism is regarded as a bourgeois affectation on the part of a liberal minority. Besides, there hasn't been much demand for emancipation; it's fairly luxurious being a housewife in South Africa. With entire fleets of black staff to do almost everything bar chew your own food for you, there is plenty of time to pursue other interests. Not many middle-class whites of a certain age choose to work, however: it is of utmost importance that they stay at home and indoctrinate — sorry — spend time with their children, in case they pick up any weird ideas from the garden hand or the cook.

Besides pottering about doing the school run here, playing a game of bridge there, many so-called "progressive" women's groups pursue some sort of conscience-salving welfare work. It makes them feel bountiful and altruistic, especially since De Klerk's speech on February 2 when, henceforth, it was good to be seen to be making friendly gestures in the direction of the black communities. Take the women's group,

Kontak, for instance. "They are currently regarding black society in a very patronising way," says Lou-Marie Kruger. "They will have parties for black women. They will go and fetch them from the townships and serve them tea and cakes in their big expensive houses. Then behind their backs they'll nudge each other and say, 'Watch the silverware' . "

Or there are groups such as the Jong Dames Dynamik (the Young Dynamic Ladies) of Johannesburg. It has to be said that there is more dynamism at play in a dead goldfish. Two of the organisers sat simpering on a sofa at the Holiday Inn, talking about their "cultural" activities. "We are involved in quite a variety of subjects — conservation, for instance — and we have a national competition for the writing of children's plays." To temper all this dynamism, some nitty-gritty was called for. What about relationships, men, sex? Do the Dynamic Ladies gossip about such things when locked in sullen sisterhood at one of their meetings? There was a long silence, some stagey coughs and a good deal of shifting about on the chintz. "Oh my goodness me no," said Suzette, less orally frigid than her sulky friend. "I would never discuss any aspect of my private personal life with a girlfriend. And no, I don't believe in sex before marriage." But what about their children? Do they teach them about drugs, contraception, abortion? More writhing about. "All our projects reflect our affiliation with the church and its moral values. Our community's still very conservative. We can teach our children to make up their own minds in life, while keeping all those ghastly, awful things out of it."

There is a young off-shoot of the dynamic ladies too, operating at Pretoria University. They do mind-bendingly girly, cheer-leaderish things like showing their solidarity with the army by sending soldiers scented love letters and giving them chocolates and flowers on Valentine's Day. Or they choose a day in the week when they will, for no apparent reason, all dress in the same colour of clothes. Hedwig Berry is the long-suffering head of a women's group at the university, thought to be fighting a losing battle against the staunch conservatism that prevails. She is forced to observe all these displays of simpering nationalistic girlishness. "There's an old joke on campus," she says, "that girls attend Pretoria University to do a BA in marriage and husband-seeking."

In the light of a changing South Africa, some women's groups are making what they regard as progressive, pioneering steps to strengthen family and community life in preparation for a more integrated society. But far-right women's groups fear a future of black rule in the country. The Kappie Kommandos — a vicious, militant minority group — are fronted by a terrifying woman called Marie van Zyl. Their motto is, "It's better to die on the right than live on the left."

But of all the Big White Mothers who suckle and nurture Afrikaner society, Anna Boshoff of the Afrikanervolkswag — daughter of the late tyrannical Calvinist prime minister, Dr Hendrik Verwoerd — is volksmoeder supreme. She has a plump face, flowery frock and a Charlotte Brontë chignon suffering severe landslide. Her office is a wistful shrine to Afrikanerdom; ornamental ox wagons as far as the eye can see, a statue of her father and cushions appliquéd with the Volkswag's logo, a fascistic juxtaposition of Vs and Ws. On the wall is a plaque with their motto, "Op trek na ons eie" — we are trekking to our own. "We are convinced that we'll never find the solution here, so the foothold of the new Afrikaner nation will have to be found in a new area. So we are working to get our people to consolidate an area in the north-western Cape, around the Orange River." The Voortrekkers embark on countrywide tours to recruit more "pioneers" to participate in the plan to build a new land. In the driveway are five sinister looking vehicles with sort of Ku Klux Klan hood-shaped backs to them. "A lot of people are worried about the future. We aren't against the blacks, but we don't believe the melting pot idea will work. We say that as Afrikaners we have a right to our own land. We are working for the future of the white man in this country."

21 Love in the shadows

Judy Rumbold

MUNGO, the gay tarot card reader of Johannesburg, has a neat theory concerning apartheid. Meat-eaters are to blame. "Their palates are on a destruction course to hell. The human carnivore will always suffer. He's filling his body with corpses and carcasses and mucus-forming trash. The body breaks down, irritability and negativity set in, and he murders his neighbour. Most criminals are carnivores".

Coincidentally, after a week's visit to South Africa, the enduring image of affluent white middle-class society was of a slab of steak being slapped on to a braai (barbecue) and the smell of char-grill suffusing the early evening air. The South Africans are inordinately fond of their braais; they'd barbecue their cornflakes if they could.

Once, General Motors South Africa mounted a hugely successful advertising campaign for Chevrolet based around the slogan, "Braaivleis, rugby, sunny skies and Chevrolet". Wine, women and song are traditionally second division stuff compared to the seductive lure of a lamb chop and a kickaround with the lads. Afrikaner men fit beautifully into this butch scenario, every one a sun-baked Adonis in shorts and a light basting of sweat. Their wives are models of blonde compliance; they have big hair, hundreds of teeth and "I love Cheerleaders" stickers in the back windows of their cars. They are, for better or worse, some of the unsexiest people in the world.

Imagine being homosexual in the midst of all this beefed-up manhood, where patriarchy, puritanism and the great phallic rise of the Dutch Reformed church spire make even the subject of heterosexual sex an undesirable notion outside marriage. Not for nothing does the only sex shop in Johannesburg advertise itself as "Joybar — sexy things for shy people".

Against this backdrop of retentive frigidity, the guardians of Calvinist morality in South Africa look more disdainfully than most upon homosexuality, which is still illegal and punishable by several years in prison, although there is no specific law to deal with it. Instead, under section 13 of the Immorality Act, sodomy is prohibited. But evidence is necessary. The police get round it by making spurious arrests for child molestation and loitering. They prosecute 250 people a year on such charges, all of them gay.

The government balks at public displays of homosexuality, however vague. The episode of Dallas featuring Stephen Carrington de-closetting was unceremoniously cut from the government-controlled SABC's schedule. It was said to contain "explicit scenes about homosexuality which might cause offence to viewers". Funny that, considering the closest Stephen got to steamy deep-throatedness was "Gee dad, I still love you, you know that". Johannesburg's only gay newspaper, Exit, has been repeatedly banned for "promoting undesirable educational material". The most recent objection raised the subject of offensive language on its lonely hearts page. Consequently the purportedly deviant words "well-hung" were replaced by "exceptionally gifted".

Exit has a circulation of 15,000 and as a representative publication it is held in mixed regard by the gay community. It has a gauche, unsophisticated tone — "Don't miss our fabulous page 4 hunk!" — but the main complaint has to do with its links with the now defunct Gasa (Gay Association of South Africa), which had a reputation as a right-wing male organisation. Now Karen Lotter, the paper's new editor, hopes to broaden Exit's readership, especially to embrace lesbians, although the lonely hearts column is still replete with requests for bearded macho men, spookily reminiscent of the nationalistic, sunny skies and braaivleis prototype.

But in a country where, in left-wing and progressive circles, the question of the "total struggle" eclipses all others, what hope is there for a liberated future for gays and lesbians in South Africa, both white and black, the oppressed and the sub-oppressed?

In Johannesburg, the gay community seem a subdued lot, with little of the sophistication, camped-up narcissism and ebullience that exists in more liberal societies. It is as though they have been de-sexualised by the political issue and by the necessity, as a Johannesburg journalist put it, to "love in the shadows". Suitably shady venues — Garbo's, The Camel's Back, Skyline and Connections — are concentrated in Hillbrow, a buzzing Soho of a place, its reputation as a relatively easy-going, mixed race area temporarily besmirched by a necklacing which took place a few weeks ago.

The most radical the cabaret scene seemed to get, however, was at Club 58, where a low-rent desert island was mocked up on stage and bawdy singers in hula-hula skirts sang lewdly about bunches of bananas and ripe melons.

The gay community seems split in its ideas of how best to mobilise the quest for greater acceptance and recognition. Some groups like Glow (Gay and Lesbian Organisation of the Witwatersrand) have actively political members belonging to the ANC, the UDF and the PAC. Besides the braaivleis, the other sure thing in South Africa is an acronym for every occasion. Glow believe that all forms of oppression must knit their way in to the one, tangled whole.

Meanwhile Body Positive, a gay support group for HIV and Aids sufferers is preoccupied with the growing threat of Aids to their community (although Aids in South Africa is a predominantly heterosexual disease). There are 300 full-blown Aids sufferers in the country, and it is estimated that close to 200,000 people may already be infected with HIV.

Johann van Rooy, the group's co-ordinator and himself an Aids sufferer, is intolerant of gay organisations such as Glow. "We haven't got time to worry about the political issue, about apartheid and what is happening to this country. Aids is more important."

Simon Nkoli, chairperson of Glow, says none will be free, until all are free. "In South Africa, gay liberation is charged with distracting from the struggle for a democratic, non-racial future. The same charges used to be levelled at the women's movement. In the struggle against oppression, Glow aims to enhance, not divide the offensive."

Nkoli is no stranger to struggle. Being born both black and gay in a country like South Africa would seem to be more bad luck than anyone ever deserved. But that's not all. In the Delmas treason trial (he was arrested in 1984 when marching as a student in protest against rent increases in the Transvaal), he was eventually acquitted after spending three years in prison. Gasa failed to support him during the trial, so he left the organisation to form Glow, originally set up to provide counselling for gays in the townships.

In these areas, special problems exist. "There are a lot of black lesbian women who are the most oppressed people in society", says Nkoli. "Many of our members have been married — forced into the situation by cultural pressures." And there is a high incidence of rape. "The macho men think that the way to change a lesbian is to force her to have sex."

Nkoli's parents thought that the best way to cure his "disease" was through visits to the local witchdoctor for a course of herbs and potions that would "make the evil go away". Then followed a consultation with a psychologist. "Fortunately, he was gay himself and he gave me a note saying 'This is to certify that Simon Nkoli is 100 per cent homosexual'."

Now Nkoli is a high-profile gay rights activist. He travels all over the world giving lectures on Glow and its role in South Africa's political struggle. But he is not without his detractors in the organised white gay community. "They're very resistant to him", says Karen Lotter. "They think he's a precocious little black who's jumped on the bandwagon. They refuse to recognise him." Van Rooy thinks that, in the absence of any substantial government funding for HIV and Aids, the kind of finance Nkoli raises as a result of his visits overseas would be better spent supporting Aids sufferers. In South Africa, AZT is not available unless patients pay for it, at R537 a month (about £120). Van Rooy lives on a state allowance of R240 per month. There is a reluctance to recognise Aids as a disease, although government-run hospitals will treat symptoms. "I was getting Alpha Interferon for my Kaposi's sarcoma, at a cost of about R6,000 a month", he says. "They didn't mind giving me that, because Kaposi's sarcoma could be construed as cancer. Then I told them I wanted AZT instead of Interferon, which didn't help that much. The next thing I knew they'd stopped the Interferon. Now there is nothing".

Ultimately, says Van Rooy, the government should be taking a more responsible attitude to its Aids education campaigns. "Here, if you even say the word condom, it's a problem. The government's campaign is all about *not* promoting condoms, because that smacks of promiscuity. They concentrate on pushing the idea of sexual fidelity and the nuclear family — in their opinion that's the only way to combat Aids."

On a sinister note, Van Rooy thinks there is a possibility that the government might be seeing Aids as a racial solution to politics in South Africa, and withholding funds as part of a macabre plot. Their meagre efforts in not promoting condoms has been successful in that it has been a complete failure.

Cultural attitudes towards sex and contraception have not helped. With the campaign aimed at whites, there were serious mistakes on the posters distributed in their areas. "Aids is Here," they read. "Heer" is

Afrikaner for "God" — which made it seem too close to a tasteless pun. Uproar ensued and, needless to say, the campaign didn't take off.

The poster designed for the black communities, on the other hand, showed a coffin being lowered into a grave in the middle of a big open field. Of course this bred stigmatisation and fear. In the black communities, with a low level of literacy, it has proved almost impossible to conduct Aids education.

Dennis Shifris is a Johannesburg GP who is active in Aids treatment and research in South Africa. "With blacks, Aids is a political thing. It's a white man's disease. And because it is invisible in its early stages (few blacks have actually contracted full-blown Aids yet) they won't believe it will kill them. They can't put a face to it."

In black sections of South African society, says Shifris, it is taboo to talk about sex. "There aren't words that are polite in the language for penis, vagina and sperm, so how do you get the message across?"

In travelling to Aids conventions all over the world, Shifris has confronted unexpected difficulties. "In this field we have a very difficult job. We are being shunned by all the international organisations because we're white South Africans. Not all white South Africans are racist pigs; there are a lot of people, white and black, who are working for the cause."

The new Township Aids Project in Soweto aims to address some of the problems associated with the voracious spread of HIV and Aids among heterosexual blacks and migrant workers. Also, Refiloe Serote, the co-ordinator, says there must be an education programme for the educators before they can even start.

"There is a high level of ignorance regarding Aids. Social workers in townships think that if you amputate the offending part of the body then the disease will go away." And in Johannesburg, she says, some of the hospital workers treating HIV sufferers wear spacesuits just to take their temperatures.

Apart from a general lack of funding, Aids education in South Africa has been hindered by numerous smear campaigns. There was fear among Indian communities recently when a pamphlet advising black men to have sex with Indian women hit the streets of Pretoria, Laudium, parts of the Transvaal, and Natal. Purporting to come from the ANC, the inflammatory pamphlet said an Aids expert had proved Indian women carried antibodies to the Aids virus, and black men should therefore choose them as sexual partners. It claimed South Africa paid Israeli scientists R1 billion for the virus, and "white racists" were using it as a slander campaign.

But it is a measure of official neglect of Aids that last year, when Body Positive campaigned for more funds from the government, they were comprehensively shunned. At the same time, there was an appeal to save the black rhino. The government matched rand for rand everything the public gave. Millions were raised. It is tempting to think that the total would have been even higher had the rhino been white.

22 *Township Fever*

Michael Billington

MY FIRST image of downtown Johannesburg was like a mirage. On a vast car park opposite the Market Theatre, a flea market was in full swing. Everything from ostrich eggs and ceramic paper bags to jewellery, paintings and books seemed to be on sale. Blacks, whites, Coloureds traded, kissed, commingled and drank together in the café-restaurant opposite the theatre. It might have been Camden Lock on a Saturday. This was South Africa?

By six o'clock that evening the mirage had disappeared: the site had been cleared and a solitary black cleaner was sweeping away the debris. The Saturday flea market is indeed both a dream and a reality. It is, I was confidently told, the one place in South Africa where all races unselfconsciously meet: a transient vision of a future possibility. But it also has a hard economic purpose: the world-renowned but totally unsubsidised Market Theatre lives off its box office and the rents (R24 a day, less than £5.50) it charges stall-holders. As John Kani, the legendary actor and associate director at the Market told me, "We are more famous than rich. Take away the flea market and we close the next Monday."

Founded in 1974 by a group led by Barney Simon and Mannie Manim, the Market is the hub of theatrical life in Johannesburg. Because of the protest nature of the work it has exported to London and Edinburgh (including Woza Albert, Poppie Nongena, Asinamali and Born In The RSA), I expected it to have the furtive shadiness of a fringe theatre. In fact it is housed in the old Indian Fruit Market — a huge, octagonal building with massive steel arches, porticoed entrance and Oriental domes.

The building contains three theatres, a bar, a restaurant, a gallery and a second-hand bookshop. Signs inside proclaiming "No poultry may be removed from the market without permission from the State Veterinarian" remind you of the building's commercial origin; a cabaret space and a jazz club dotted around the flagstoned courtyard at the front of the Market testify to its recent expansiveness. Imagine the original Covent Garden turned into a community centre rather than chic tourist trap and you get the picture.

But the Market Theatre occupies a paradoxical position in South African life. It has become a focus of opposition to a discredited system. Its plays have frequently fallen foul of the Censorship Board (in the case of Spike Milligan's The Bed Sitting Room because the divinity was familiarly referred to as "Goddie").

It plays to a genuinely mixed clientele, though the black audience that can afford its R15 top price tends to come at the end of the week, around pay day. It reaches out to the community through its Laboratory, which offers advice and help to township groups. Yet, as John Kani pointed out, government officials show foreign visitors round to demonstrate their ostensible liberalism. The Market is both a liberated zone in a divided city (the white suburbs to the north and Soweto to the south could be on different planets) and a symbol of what Marcuse called "repressive tolerance".

But whether the Market Theatre is heroic survivor or safety valve, it has an exemplary record of opposition to apartheid. Which makes it all the more ironic that its current main-house production, Township Fever, has come under attack not from the ruling National Party but from black opposition groups.

Presented by a company called Committed Artists, the show is written, directed and choreographed by Mbongeni Ngema, whose credits include Woza Albert, Asinamli and the hit musical Sarafina. In the furore about Township Fever, the arguments against it boil down to two: that it misrepresents the 1987 railway workers' strike that is its subject, and that it is aimed more for Broadway export than for local consumption.

My own feeling is that Ngema has tried to do the impossible: write a musical that is simultaneously a celebration of township life and a condemnation of a system that pits worker against worker. His theme is an historic strike that paralysed South African Transport, a cornerstone of apartheid, but that also led to four scabs being killed by fellow workers on the night of April 28, 1987. The subject cries out for sober documentary treatment: what it gets is a periodically upbeat musical, as if Andrew Lloyd Webber had gone into partnership with Tariq Ali.

Beginning on Death Row, where four of the 18 workers involved are still awaiting execution, the show takes the form of a prolonged flashback. It focuses on the fortunes of Jazz Mngadi who wants to be a township musician, is impelled by his mother to take a job on the railways and, through economic desperation, is driven to attack a fellow worker.

The problem is that slabs of expertly drilled song-and-dance (including a frenzied New Year's feast and a rainbow-hued township wedding) are followed by slabs of gritty realism: the music does not so much propel the tragedy as impede it. And although the show's heart is in the right place (in its attack on the death penalty as a legacy of apartheid) it fails to explain that the scab-murders took place in the context of appalling police violence.

It is, however, a measure of the extent to which theatre matters in a non-democratic society, that the show has aroused such controversy. Knowing that he was dealing with a sensitive issue, Ngema invited members of the union-based Living Wage Group to witness rehearsals in order to explain how he had used artistic licence in matters such as the election of a shop steward. This did not, however, prevent the Cultural Desk, an alliance of artistic organisations set up by the United Democratic Front, from asking Mr Ngema to "review" certain scenes, nor did it stop the play getting a roasting in the influential weekly, New Nation.

John Kani says the controversy has been played up by the conservative press: doubtless true, but I also saw for myself a noisy street fracas between members of Committed Artists and a rival theatrical group. What this proves is that art is inseparable from politics in South Africa. As Ian Steadman, professor of drama at the University of the Witwatersrand, pointed out to me, "Theatre in South Africa has frequently functioned as a newspaper, bringing out the facts of economic and social life. It has also gained much of its strength and energy in the last 15 years from its moral opposition to apartheid. As that system crumbles, people will have to scramble around to find other targets."

Proof of what Steadman says about the political power of theatre in South Africa is everywhere to hand. Of 13 defendants brought to court under the Terrorism Act in March 1975, five were well-known theatre practitioners. A Black Consciousness theatre has burgeoned in churches, community halls and cellars in Soweto (where there are no official theatres) producing notable work by writers like Maishe Maponya and Matsemela Manaka. And since 1980 a flourishing trade union theatre movement has grown up. It all started apparently when a lawyer representing the Metal and Allied Workers Union asked its members to dramatise an issue he didn't understand: this grew into a play, Ilanga or The Sun Will Rise, that became a model for educational-agitational unionised theatre. We look to drama for uplift and diversion: in South Africa it is an instrument of change.

Albie Sachs, a long-standing ANC campaigner, triggered off a major debate in South Africa by suggesting that the phrase "culture as a weapon of struggle" should be banned for five years. As an outsider, what strikes me is that that will only be possible in a truly post-apartheid society. John Kani, through his work with Athol Fugard has done as much as anyone to advance the cause of art. But he points out that when he goes home at night to Soweto he has to drive through three road blocks and enter a world where street lights are scarce, where his son has grown up to treat an army tank as a toy and where, professionally, he himself has never appeared on the main South African TV network. As he says, "It is understandable that black work is full of pain and anger and has even assumed the title of protest theatre. Actually, it is not protest: it is simply a record of what is happening to people in their everyday lives."

The Market Theatre, of which John Kani is a vital part, has a long and honourable record of opposition. But, it strikes me, arriving in South Africa on a short-term visit, that only when the kind of relaxed integration I saw both at the Saturday flea market and around the Market Theatre is the norm, rather than an aberration, will it be possible for drama to reach beyond reportage, education and protest. For the moment, it still has imperative work to do in the world.

23 A role for theatre

Michael Billington

TO BOYCOTT or not to boycott? That is the burning question. Do we keep up cultural sanctions on South Africa at a time of limited change? Both British Actors' Equity and the Writers' Guild say it is up to the individual conscience: in fact, no British drama is seen on South African TV screens (an Equity members' decision which Marius Goring intends to challenge in the courts) and the majority of British playwrights refuse to let their work be done on stage. There are well-known South African opponents of the boycott, including André Brink and Helen Suzman. However, the message I kept getting from the Johannesburg arts scene was "keep up the pressure".

In fact, the official ANC and UDF line on the boycott is subtly changing. In 1987 the Dutch government hosted a conference of anti-apartheid groups at which it was agreed to maintain the boycott while agreeing to "progressive exchanges." Mzwakhe Mabuli, a charismatic poet-musician organises the Cultural Desk from a hectic downtown Johannesburg office, where a picture of Mike Tyson is pinned up alongside one of Nelson Mandela. Mr Mabuli told me: "In the past, the boycott was a blunt instrument. It was not meant to harm people already oppressed but to advance the anti-apartheid cause. But it has had a decisive effect on the government, particularly when taken in conjunction with economic and sporting sanctions, as you can see from their pathetic plea to exiled artists to return home. Not even in the foreseeable future should the boycott be relaxed, particularly when the Maggie Thatchers of this world are calling for the lifting of financial sanctions."

But what do "progressive exchanges" mean? Actor-director John Kani, who passionately supports the boycott, explained how it can be used selectively. "Beckett allowed us to do Catastrophe because it was written for Vaclav Havel as a protest against the persecuted artist. Pinter permitted us to do One For The Road because it deals with torture in a repressive state. But the point is that we in South Africa should be the people to decide because we can read the situation here. We pleaded with Pinter to let us do his play because it is an incredible piece. And instead of having a white security man interrogating a black family, I played the security boss investigating a white family. It had an amazing effect. As soon as it opened, whites were walking out of the bloody theatre. Black audiences loved it: they said it feels good for once to be on the other side of the fence. But the black press saw the point, which is that Pinter's play warns us that power corrupts, regardless of skin colour."

What is fascinating is the intensity of the debate about the cultural boycott: every night, after the play, we would sit in theatre-bars discussing it (there is little small-talk in South Africa). Many remarks lin-

A ROLE FOR THEATRE

ger in the mind. "It has hit popular music more than anything else. A whole generation grew up never having seen the Beatles, the Stones or Bob Dylan in concert" (Junction Theatre director Malcolm Purky). "It has slightly stunted the broad development of the arts in South Africa" (Market Theatre director Janice Honeyman). "It has produced a whole new wave of local writers and boosted South African theatre" (actress Vanessa Cooke). "The real deprivation has not been missing out on work from Europe but from the rest of the African continent" (drama and dance critic Adrienne Sichel). John Kani, however, put it well: "As soon as a commitment is made to creating a better South Africa for all, then the doors will have to be opened." The message I got from the majority was clear: having kept up the boycott for so long, it would be pointless to relax it now.

WE ALL KNOW that FW de Klerk is terrified of state socialism. Intriguing to discover, therefore, that the government accepts the principle of state subsidy for the arts. Each of the four provinces has its own "independent, autonomous" Performing Arts Council (the one for the Transvaal is called PACT) which administers funds and acts as a producing company: the total subsidy for the performing arts for 1988-89 was around R65 million (£14.7 million) of which PACT received a third.

How is subsidy determined? By objective statistics rather than subjective judgments. The South Africans have devised a curious method of "formula financing" by which bums-on-seats are multiplied by hours of attendance. All very Thatcherite. The logic of that method would seem to be that a long farce would get you more money than a short tragedy: what price Sophocles? But, to be fair, PACT's current programme includes Fidelio, La Traviata, King Lear (in Afrikaans), The Seagull, Animal Farm and the ballet Don Quixote. Subsidy, however, has its own catch-22. Because the central government is strapped for cash, it can't stump up the expected funds: so PACT is getting only 65 per cent of the sum to which it is statistically entitled. Sounds familiar.

Dennis Reinecke, ex-opera singer and PACT's deputy chief director, occupies a baronial Pretoria office dominated by a bust of Paul Kruger and points up the amount of work done: 2,200 performances per annum of opera, drama, dance, music and ballet. Of course, PACT is officially integrated. But how much work is there by and for blacks? Over to Mr Reinecke: "The process of bringing first-world culture into a Third World situation is inevitably going to take time. But when we did Aida we had a black artist, Martina Arroyo, in the lead and the Ethiopian Chorus was entirely black. Thirty-five per cent of our contemporary dance company and our opera chorus is black, we have six black actors in our drama company, we have taken an educational opera project, The Milkbird, to the black community, we have sent an Indian dance company on tour and we have one black, one Coloured and one Indian on our board."

To Mr Reinecke, this is progress: to me, it sounds like tokenism. PACT undeniably does some interesting work. In Johannesburg at the Windybrow Theatre Centre (a green-and-white neo-colonial building that resembles a Surrey golf club), I caught three short plays in their Pot Pourri festival of new work: the best, Angel In A Dark Room by Aletta Bezuidenhout, darkly hinted at a lesbian relationship between a white photographer and her black model. But, in two evenings at the Windybrow, I saw just the one black on stage and none in the audience. Mr Reinecke talks of "educating" the black audience. Why not acknowledge the humming vitality of its own existing culture?

I HAD two experiences which confirmed my point; and did something more. One afternoon I went to a run-through of Street Sisters: a musical about prostitution in the Johannesburg district of Hillbrow mounted by The Mamu Players (their first show, Township Boy, played at the ICA last year). I was ushered into a derelict, downtown warehouse where the company of 35 actors and musicians had erected their own stage and lived, loved and worked together in an orderly commune. John Ledwaba (writer, director and lyricist) and Christo Leach (producer) announced auditions a year ago in the black press: a thousand young people turned up from the townships in the Eastern Cape, Natal and Soweto. Of those chosen, only four had ever been on stage and some spoke limited English. After eight months' intensive work, they had been turned into a fine-tuned ensemble.

The show itself was funny, abrasive, informative, tuneful (excellent music by Lionel Summithram) and overlong: at three-and-a-half hours it needed, and will get, drastic pruning. But it said a lot about the social origins of black prostitution (one girl had been set up by her father because he wanted her road-tested before he claimed her bride-price) and treated the women as peculiarly resilient victims rather than jolly exotics or sentimental waifs. What struck me, however, was the energy and dedication of the performers.

A year ago, as someone said, they were "damaged" products of township life. Now they are set to open at the Grahamstown Festival (South Africa's Edinburgh) in late June and then go on tour to Germany, Holland and Belgium. The show was good: more importantly, it had given its young actors status, self-definition and hope.

I saw a similar process at work in Soweto. One thundery night I accompanied the Market Theatre Laboratory's field-group on a trip to the YMCA at Orlando in Soweto to see work in a progress on a show called Children of the Ghetto. The Lab, under Mark Fleishman and James Mtoba, offers practical advice to some 17 community groups around Johannesburg. This is not paternalism: they go only where asked. Organised by a skilled choreographer (Jackie Semela who works by day as a bank cashier), the company they were visiting was a dance-based troupe that wanted help with drama. Sitting in a grim, orange-walled room, I watched as Fleishman, a graduate of the University of Cape Town working in a patient, Peter Brookish way, set up improvisations based on village life: unselfconsciously, these young townees transformed themselves into trees, birds, rocks, tortoises, even a chattering monkey. An African village suddenly came to life before our eyes.

Afterwards, we talked. I learned that each weeknight they rehearse in the YMCA from 5.30 till 7.30 and perform at weekends. Only one wanted to go into showbiz. Of the others, one got up at 4.30 each morning to drive a taxi, another worked in a storeroom, two were part-time students, another two had started their own design-firm (Fancol) specialising in invitation-cards. I asked one of them what he really wanted to design: "textiles, stage-sets, motor cars," was the ambitious answer. All came from poor homes: all were determined to get on. Doing theatre for them was not just a random pastime: it was a vital means of self-expression and a way of acquiring their own voice. On a wet, gloomy night in Soweto, I felt that rarest of all sensations in South Africa: a sudden charge of optimism.

24 Poem

Into the skin
Lionel Abrahams

My way into you, stranger-neighbour,
is not to ask the way:
no instruction can lead me,
and nor can I practise or think
or feel my way in to be black or a woman,
victim or addict of blood
or money or prayer.

The other I become
becomes itself in perilous luck,
spawn of nullity and thought,
lust with nothing to do but lust;
this is how the monster is born,
the criminal occurs.

And this is the fantastic grace:
the flames of viciousness
have burned me tenderly
into your skin.

25 Stolen lives

Ian Mayes

*The muck, the smell, the fortitude, despair, endurance.
Always the sounds begin again.*
  — *Es'kia Mphahlele: Afrika My Music, 1984*

Come on over . . . let us talk.
  — *Es'kia Mphahlele: Renewal Time, 1981*

THIS is far enough from Johannesburg. Let Soweto begin. Es'kia Mphahlele, now 70, runs the Council for Black Education and Research at the Funda Centre, a cultural and educational enterprise on the edge of the township. Not far down the road is one of Soweto's squatter camps. There is nothing to be said in the face of such a place. In this abominable jumble thousands of people live precarious lives in precarious homes, patched together from oddments of corrugated iron, wood, fabric. An indescribable stink rises from it. This is part of the context in which South African writers write. Can they now, in the new atmosphere of hope, raise their eyes from such scenes, stand back from direct engagement in the struggle and, guiltlessly, explore the full range of human emotion and character?

The debate is not a new one, but it has been intensified within South Africa by an influential member of the ANC, the writer Albie Sachs. He has suggested that members of the ANC should be banned from saying that culture is a weapon of struggle. "In the first place," he says, "it results in an impoverishment of our art. Instead of getting real criticism, we get solidarity criticism." And he asserts: "Culture is not something separate from the general struggle ... Culture is us, it is who we are, how we see ourselves and the vision we have of the world."

Mphahlele is familiar with this debate — indeed, he foreshadowed it in his autobiography, Down Second Avenue, written in the late 1950s when he had his first taste of freedom in Nigeria at the beginning of nearly 20 years of exile. This book, in which he reclaimed his life from the grip of apartheid, was among the very first autobiographies by a black South African and is still among the most successful. It has been translated into Bulgarian, Czech, Serbo-Croat, Russian, German, French, Italian, Japanese and Hebrew.

"Not all of us have invested everything we had in 'protest literature'. Many of us have tried to write about other things besides oppression," he says. "People still fall in love. People still make love. People are still born. People die. People still betray one another. I have always felt that in my writing I must not be bullied by our kind of protest formula, but that I must reach out to other areas of the human drama. It doesn't mean that you do that to the exclusion of the socio-political context, because you can't. People live in the context that has been assigned to them and in this country we lead lives that we would not otherwise live. What I'm saying is that one orchestrates the single melody of protest with so many other things in the human drama — that is not getting away from it, that is not living in the clouds. There is a host of readers out there who are not just contented with being told they are in big trouble, that they are living under tyranny."

Down Second Avenue provides an interesting commentary on the way the literary censorship system — now much relaxed — still twitches. The book was immediately banned when it came out in a comic version for children a couple of years ago. Perhaps the objection was to cartoon frames that dealt with Mphahlele's period as a journalist and literary editor on Drum magazine, covering the Sophiatown evictions and the township resistance to Bantu education.

Mphahlele says, "It was banned because it gave access to a larger public, to children and because it speaks directly in pictures which are vivid illustrations of this sordid environment." Now it is unbanned but distribution is restricted to bookshops. It may not be sold informally, that is by activists at meetings, rallies or cultural events where sales of greater significance might be achieved.

Mphahlele has mixed feelings about the apparent changes in South African society and remains sceptical about the government's intentions. "You ask yourself, what makes them do this? Apart from sanctions, external pressures and so on, what is it? Is it a moral thing, a moral itch, is it the turning of a conscience? What is it? I keep asking myself." Nevertheless, he believes that writers should now be creating a base for a leap ahead into the future, "taking people beyond the instant and letting them know who they are and where they come from."

"The writer now certainly has to be free. I mean, the black Americans are like that. Over decades through the civil rights movement and their own kind of protest they have emerged just brilliantly."

LATER that day I am with the novelist Nadine Gordimer, who is closely involved in the work of the Congress of South African Writers, a non-racial organisation dedicated among other things to tending the grassroots of literary culture. We talk as the light fades in the garden of her home in the white suburbs of Johannesburg. We are a long way from the stench of the squatter camps in the interstices of Soweto.

"I think writing was a part of the struggle and contributed to the struggle and will continue to contribute to the struggle to keep us free. But I think it is time for it to come out of battledress — and some of us have really kept it that way all along. I mean Njabulo Ndebele is one of them. It may not seem daring to you but in that book of his, Fools [a collection of stories which won the Noma Award for publishing in Africa in 1983] he wrote about childhood at a time when writers were thinking, no, if I write about that kind of thing I'm going to be told I'm not contributing to the liberation struggle. And young, particularly young black writers, felt it very strongly. They didn't have the self-confidence to understand that if you are a black writer and you are writing about the kind of childhood that you had, then it's a political statement because the way that you lived was the result of apartheid. You don't have to choose characters who are totally stylised. There was a time, for instance, when if a black writer was describing a family relationship, the mother was always the most wonderful figure, an absolute saint. It could never be that the mother was a bitch and a pain in the neck and totally inhibiting the life of her children. She had to be the great black mother. Similarly every policeman had to be a monster. There was a kind of standard way of dealing with characters."

Ndebele himself explained what he tried to do in Fools, when I met him during a brief visit to Oxford. "Basically, the intention was deliberately to free the reader from the expectation that when you open a book and you start reading you are going to find reflected the traditional conflict between white and black. Not that this conflict doesn't have a legitimacy of its own. But what has happened over the years is that the conflict has preoccupied the imagination of people almost to the total exclusion of other concerns.

"So the book was an attempt on my part to focus attention on the quality of life in its creative aspects in the townships of South Africa. It seemed to me that that would go some way towards consolidating the very important sense of community which is beyond the easy manipulations of the system."

Ndebele, who holds a high-ranking post at the University of Lesotho, is the president of the Congress of South African Writers (Cosaw), but was unable to be at the special executive meeting of the organisation that I attended in Cape Town because of difficulties with the South African authorities. He has lived in Lesotho since 1969, has been a naturalised citizen of that country since 1979 and needs a visa every time he enters South Africa. He has recently been appointed vice-rector of the University of Western Cape but so far the South African government has refused the work permit that would enable him to take up the appointment. "One can only speculate about the reasons. It is possible that they don't like the idea that a black person should occupy a position of such seniority in a university that was meant to be for Coloured people."

SO THE Cosaw executive meeting, held in a community building a bit like a YMCA, goes on without him and during the lunch break, I talk to some of the members. The discussion starts with a laugh. I ask what they see as the particular reasons for optimism at the moment. Achmat Dangor, poet and novelist, the author of Waiting For Leila, says, "We're going to have an ANC government next month." But as the conversation gets going it reflects the dilemma and the challenge that Cosaw faces in its attempts to discover and develop rising talent. It is tilling a field long left untended, and throwing itself with impressive passion at problems of language and literacy compounded by an education system that stinks. And it is trying to help aspirant women writers, who in many ways are worst off. Nise Malange believes a start has been made through Cosaw workshops in the townships and rural areas. "It is," she says, "one of our priorities." Because Cosaw is nearer the action, it is also in the frontline of arguments about standards, about "fine" and "rough" writing and degrees of overt political engagement.

Junaid Ahmed, a poet, says, "There has been a flood of writing of what you could call political slogans, in prose and poetry, and that has formed a necessary part of the liberation struggle. But we are concerned that we do not get trapped in this form of writing, so what we are addressing is how to transform it into art." Another poet, Buyisile Jonas, puts it like this, "We should look, through our writings, at what tomorrow should be like and not necessarily write about the flag that should be hoisted now."

Much of the discussion is taken up with the issue of language. "We are encouraging people not to feel obliged to communicate their opinions through English," says Jonas. Dangor adds: "We have to overcome a kind of cultural snobbery, imposed on us, historically, by those who have said you must write and publish in English. It means that people mutilate their work by artificially translating it themselves into English."

Ahmed: "One of the most interesting things coming out of the work of young aspirant writers is a fusion of languages, where one writes not necessarily in English, or solely in Sotho or whatever, but with sometimes six different languages in one poem."

Dangor: "The mixture of languages is unbelievable. You could almost say it's a cultural lingua franca, where people will speak English but write in this curious mixed language. Many of us here, apart from the purists, write in that language ourselves, and I would find it very difficult to write in pure English."

The novelist, Mewa Ramgobin, author of Waiting To Live, says, "South Africa is going through a trauma and our literature reflects this. It catches the moment, it mobilises and it leads. That is why censorship has been so fundamentally important to the state. It had to restrict the free flow of ideas." Junaid Ahmed adds: "We must make the point that we are not ideology-bound. We accommodate people from broad ideological positions, whether from Black Consciousness, the ANC, or wherever, and we have managed to do this very successfully in the past two or three years."

The ferment at this level is head-spinning. I emerge into the driving rain of an autumn in Cape Town. Table Mountain is two-thirds shrouded in its table cloth of cloud. The publisher who is showing me round says: "See it as a metaphor for South African Society."

BACK IN THE suburbs of Johannesburg with the critic, poet, editor and publisher, Lionel Abrahams, whose poetry has an acerbity and sense of irony the absence of which, you might say, is one of the distinguishing features of the apartheid regime. Early on he wrote The Whiteman Blues, which opens:

Two cars, three loos, a swimming pool,
investment paintings, kids at private school . . .
we entertain with shows of gourmet food —
and yet we don't feel right, we don't feel good.

And later on he wrote The Old Man Blues which begins:

The old man doesn't go out much any more.
He's rather losing touch.

He has a personal abhorrence of committees. "There is a strangulation of intellectual and cultural life in the townships because of the committee system that people are bound to get involved with." And he shares an anxiety, expressed by others, that writers in South Africa, having once got rid of censorship from the right, should not be subjected to censorship from the left. Nadine Gordimer on the same theme had said: "I think this is what Albie Sachs is pleading for — that once we get rid of apartheid and once we get rid of the moral and political strictures present now, that loyalty to the future regime should not tell us what to write."

Abrahams points directly at the Cultural Desk, an office set up in Johannesburg by the United Democratic Front to co-ordinate the efforts of the various cultural bodies seeking to make the most of the apparently changed atmosphere. "The Cultural Desk exists to implement a policy of selective boycott. South African artists and performers intending to go abroad find themselves either encouraged or hampered by the Cultural Desk, according to whether or not they are allies of the struggle." He insists, "People have the right to be irrelevant to the struggle."

It seemed a good time to bring up the question of guilt. "I wonder whether the problem of guilt isn't going to be both lighter and more complicated from now on. Lighter, because we are no longer bound to feel ourselves associated willy-nilly with a machine rolling in an evil direction. The thing isn't monolithic in that way any more. More complicated because the responsibility becomes more individual now. It's also, in a way, removing some of the pressure to profess guilt."

Guilt is a one-sided affair in South Africa, and a tiny price, you might say, if that is all that is to be paid in the aftermath of apartheid. I do not believe the last chapter in the literature of the struggle has been written, but the broken conversation may now become more coherent. With censorship a less significant interference, more people seem to hear the unjammed messages passing across the divide. One of them says, "Come on over . . . let us talk." Excuse the smell.

Down Second Avenue by Ezekiel (Es'kia) Mphahlele is published by Faber. Renewal Time is available in a Readers International edition. Mphahlele's Afrika My Music is published by Ravan Press, Johannesburg. Njabulo Ndebele's book of stories, Fools, is in the Longman African Classics series. Nadine Gordimer's most recent novel, A Sport Of Nature is published by Cape (Penguin paperback). Achmat Dangor's Waiting For Leila is published by Ravan Press in its Staffrider series. Waiting To Live by Mewa Ramgobin is published by David Philip (Cape Town). Ad Donker in Johannesburg publishes A Lionel Abrahams Reader. Most of the books are available from the Africa Book Centre, 36 King Street, Covent Garden, London WC2E 8JT (071 240 6649), which also has some of the Cosaw publications.

26 Sparks of talent

Nadine Gordimer tells Ian Mayes how she conducts a writers' workshop for Cosaw, the Congress of South African Writers

WHEN YOU go into a country district or into the black section of a mining town and you run a short story workshop there the first thing that throws you into despair is that the people are writing in English, their education is so bad, so poor, that though some of them have good ideas when they speak, they simply can't formulate them for a story.

Very often they haven't the vocabulary, never mind the grammar — no one's a stickler for grammar, you can have wonderful poetry and stories that ignore all those things — but they just haven't got the vocabulary. I know that Zeke Mphahlele [the writer and educationist Es'kia Mphahlele] who does a lot of this kind of work is in despair at the level of education of people writing in their own languages. So you have to overcome that. But if someone has a spark of talent you can still go ahead.

I'm not an academic. I don't know how to teach. I've never taught in my life. I only "teach" the way I've taught myself to write, which is to become self-critical and to read, read, read. And people don't read.

They don't have the opportunity, they haven't had the libraries — libraries have only been open to everybody for about 10 years and in some small towns they are still not open to blacks. And the schools have a few dog-eared books.

But the imagination is there. I had an interesting experience recently. I had a weekend of workshops and I did the short story one — and it was a group I had been with before so we'd done the general talking about what a short story is, taking it to pieces and seeing how it is put together. Most people bring their own stories and then they are read and everybody tears them to pieces. But you just can't write short stories unless you have some background, so that at least you know what can be done with a short story.

What I usually do is take along photocopies of three or four stories. I'm just trying to show the scope, the wonderful scope and the different things you can do. I would take for instance, Chinua Achebe — one of my favourites is his Uncle Ben story which is so funny and marvellous — then something by a local African writer, say Can Themba, someone like that, then bang in the middle would be a Chekhov and then one of my favourites, Before The Law by Kafka. Usually no one has read Kafka and some have not even heard of him, but it's an enormous success because everyone relates to him so tremendously — you know, people are always waiting in queues to get a house or to bribe somebody all those things they relate to their own lives.

But what I did having gone through that first stage — we'd looked at stories that were mainly dialogue, we'd looked at the first person story and so on — I thought what about allegory? It was then that I took along the Kafka and a little story, an anonymous story, put together by the cultural wing of Frelimo during the struggle for independence in Mozambique. So there they had one that was truly a product of group activity — I don't know who wrote it. I don't know how it was put together.

So we looked at these two. Then there's a kind of guide about how people like workshops to be run. Now no matter how you bullied me I couldn't go off with others and put together an allegorical poem or story — I would be struck dumb. Anyway they went off in three groups for less than an hour. Two of the groups came back with the most amazing allegories — really beautiful. So, you see, the imagination is there, the feeling is there. It's just the lack of education. You realise then that your codes of reference are sometimes impossible and you must abandon them. That's not patronising, it's just reality.

27 The right to read

Ian Mayes

THE MOST recent security raids of any significance on publishers in South Africa happened over a period from May to July, 1989. David Philip, the Cape Town publisher, whose titles include Detention And Torture In South Africa (Don Foster, with Dennis Davis and Diane Sadler), had four visits in six weeks. They followed a similar pattern.

"It's laughable, really. Three gentlemen arrive, one enormously tall who is there to carry the books, one medium sized and one little one who is the bright one — he's actually looking round all the time to see what there is to pick up."

Among the books seized were two imported from publishers in London: South Africa Belongs To Us, A History of the ANC by Francis Meli (published in Britain by James Currey) and Culture In Another South Africa (Zed Books). Philip has still not managed to retrieve his stock after more than a year, despite the fact that both books are now unbanned. Fortunately the numbers involved were small — about 100 copies altogether — because he follows a policy with imported books of bringing in a few initially to test the water.

"At first they were declared 'not undesirable' with the restriction that they may be bought only by university libraries. We complained and said you are having your cake and eating it. You are not incurring the odium of actually banning these books but at the same time you are, in effect, making them unavailable. In the case of the ANC book we said surely we have to start getting to know the people with whom we are dealing. Anyway we resubmitted them and this time, but after nearly a year, they were passed without any restrictions at all."

Philip, who set up his firm with his wife, Marie, in 1971, has had his own way of dealing with the restrictions. He has turned a Nelsonian blind eye to them. "You know, one of the things I made a point of not doing was to read the legislation that affected the publishing of books." He and his lawyers have preferred to grapple with problems after the event.

The small independent progressive publishers, David Philip in Cape Town, and others like the three Johannesburg houses, Ravan, Ad Donker and Skotaville have been at the sharp end of conflict with the state for up to 20 years. They have shared a common approach: when you are attacked, fight back and make as much noise about it as possible.

Now they form the core of a new organisation, the Independent Publishers Association of South Africa, IPASA. They see it as the publishers' organisation of the future and all the indications are that it will be. Something like 30 publishing houses, large and small, have already joined — all subscribing to a constitution which calls, in effect, for the scrapping of apartheid, the repeal of all repressive and discriminatory legislation, the release of prisoners of conscience and an end to censorship. One of its clauses states, "It is the belief of IPASA that a free and effective publishing industry can only exist in a democratic society, in which all citizens vote for a central legislature." Philip, as the first chairperson of IPASA, is gratified by the rush to join. "All the publishers are getting into the act now. It's competition and that's good. But one can't help asking, where have you been for the last 20 years of the struggle?"

Everyone concedes that censorship and its harassments have eased in recent years. "Books and people are coming out of prison, and that's exciting," says Philip. But no one believes the struggle is over. Andries Oliphant, the editor of Ravan Press's influential Staffrider quarterly, founded in 1978, which persisted through early bannings to become probably the most successful literary magazine the country has had, believes it is early days to assess the new situation. He says, "We are now in a transitional period and it's difficult to see how it is going to be resolved, whether by the end of apartheid or through some policy of containment. All the laws that enable them to harass journalists and publishers are still in place. There is still the possibility of regression."

Ad Donker, who has been publishing independently since the early 70s, says his euphoria after the unbanning of the ANC and the release of Mandela evaporated within a day or two. "My wife and I had second thoughts. We said it's a trap, they'll change don't you worry. No, I'm fairly pessimistic." He argues that publishers should move closer to the struggle and stay there for as long as it takes for the country to reach "true democracy".

Mothobi Mutloatse of Skotaville, the only all-black publishing house, says "We are part of the struggle whether we like it or not, as victims of white racism. We differ from the white publishers because we *are* the disenfranchised and the dispossessed. We don't separate politics from publishing." He says Skotaville was founded in 1982 "because we had to be masters of our own fate" and to try to reverse the trend in which blacks are simply consumers and not producers. "This is not an anti-white issue. It is a pro-black issue. We are not apologetic about being pro-black."

Like his colleagues in the other independents he drives on through all the state restrictions in search of new writing, in his case specifically by black writers. He has been involved in a competition, sponsored by a liquor company, to find it, but he believes the great novel by a black writer has yet to be written and may be a long, long time coming.

Ad Donker also points to the enormous handicaps that black writers face within South Africa. "Will there be a black writer with the patience to sit down while all this goes on around him? It could happen, maybe during the last few years of the decade." By then South Africa could be another country.

28 Letter to a young writer

Es'kia Mphahlele

DEAR FELLOW-DREAMER, So you want to be a writer? What writer? may I ask. Do you want to write novels and short stories? Poetry or drama? Expository prose, eg essays, public addresses, etc? Make up your mind. Now. It is not easy to try more than one within the same period of apprenticeship. You need to be committed to the one your inclination and temperament lead you to.

Whichever genre you decide on requires a commitment. I can't overemphasise this. When you have slaved for some years in your favourite medium, a whim may take you on an excursion, say out of fiction to poetry or drama. Your commitment saves you wandering all over the place trying to decide what you're really good at. Actually I'm understating the process. Rather than a whim, it is that experience, dramatic or emotional or both, that vibrates in your blood and bones: that is what will tell you to write a poem or play, etc, to explore this experience. You don't go about saying "I want an experience I can write a poem about . . ." You should have a fairly clear idea about the form of the novel, short story, drama, etc, we've inherited from the tradition of the language we are using. Words such as "poem" or "novel" are used with reference to what one has actually read. You should read, read, read in your chosen genre — items that are satisfying and those that are not so satisfying.

Early in your career characters, diction and so on will slip into your writing that come from your reading. So be it. Hack your way through the bushes till you discover your own style, one that expresses the real you. There is such a thing as a literary plot or tragedy or comedy. We produce this when we borrow other writers' emotions, anxieties, grief, humour, etc. There are also literary conventions we often pick up and must one day wean ourselves from. The same applies to figures of speech. You know the familiar metaphors, similes, hyperbole that taste like sawdust: writers must keep composing their own. Not for ornament but because the figure illuminates a point.

You're not going to wait until you have exhausted the reading list I sent you the other day before you attempt to write. It must serve as a mere guide. When you have some idea of a novel, a short story, a poem, a play (they are all represented here) you go about the business of writing. About 600 words a day, maybe a descriptive piece, narrative, or both, maybe a poem of 25-30 lines. Something. This is to develop a facility with words to start you learning how to turn real-life experience into a literary experience.

Which brings me to the point about diction — the choice of words. you know, Padi, the ancient poets who had a reputation in their communities for their gift of the spoken word chose their words carefully. They were seldom sloppy. They even seemed to be savouring words on their tastebuds! So why should we today imagine that self-expression is all we need worry about? Anyone who tells you content is more important than style is talking bullshit. You will learn in time that what you say in your writing shapes, and is shaped by, the manner of expression. you can't speak nonsense beautifully. Not really.

Work hard at your diction. There's a catch here, though. You can revise a script to death by trying too long to clean up the prose. There's one of the challenges. To refine it too vigorously can take the juice out of it, it can lose a valuable measure of the passion that launched you. Passion, Padi. Not only have you to feel passionately about your subject, but you must also breath passion into your main characters, their situations, their dialogue, their actions. The fitting diction you create brings characters, things, events and places into bold relief. Likewise if you are in verse or drama, breath into the piece of writing your own zest, your own enthusiasm.

With longer and longer training your instincts will tell you which subject calls for a novel or poem or drama or short story or essay. Remember W. H. Auden's observation that poetry is "memorable speech." Indeed this is what distinguishes good works of the imagination from exposition as a medium through which information comes to us.

You've probably read some of the verse several of our young apprentices write. Most of what they say is mere information. Especially how deep the shit is we're in. They call it "being relevant" or "committed." Can't someone whisper in their ears that if they were committed rather to their art and craft and humanity at its various levels, we might be saved the embarrassment of reading their talkative verse or plays? "Relevance" and "commitment" are used by our comrades today as if they had invented social realism or even politics. And they talk as if they had come upon a discovery as startling as that of a teenager who suddenly realises that he can sleep with a girlfriend and actually mate with her.

My warning, Padi, is that you should not be bullied by these slogans, which most often come from failed writers and failed politicians, usually at the branch level. I'd say be committed as a man among men and women, as a social being. March and demand and boycott and picket as a political animal. When you come to writing, your commitment is first and foremost to yourself, your subject, your styles of treating it, the point you want to make, your sense of community. For we all write in order to make a point. Not a didactic point, just a point about the human experience as you perceive it. Make your point damn it! There's got to be something you want to reveal or illuminate — without telling us you're doing so, of course.

Hell, there's so much one can commit oneself to. If we listened to and heeded every political baboon barking from the rocks to order writers and artists to a goose march, where would we be? I look at our comrades — My, I just admire their energy! — and what do I see when they are in a conference as aspiring writers? Frustrated, desperate non-writers bogged down in the mire of rhetoric about what they should be writing, how they should be "committed," what writers are committed, what writers are bourgeois, whom to contact overseas. Testifying, forever testifying, flailing the air with gestures that approximate a floor-thrashing seizure. Say this to yourself, brotherman, that you can train yourself to carry your curiosity forward by sharpening your powers of observation, and the desire to know more about people; listen attentively when people talk and when one tells you an anecdote. Make notes about those that your instinct tells you have a social significance. The same for newspaper reports — incidents suggest a story beneath their bare surface. There are thousands of themes in these news reports.

Stories and poems build up in my own mind, I let them spin themselves and replay the themes, still in my mind. This can last for five years or more before I commit something to writing. Most of what I do, once I've got to a start, is to try to get the thing right. Get it right: the single melody that is the story or theme and the orchestration of it. Orchestration is a way of creating resonances. For those who have invested almost everything in protest writing would do well, I think, to learn the effect of resonances: voices and actions of the surrounding terrain, historical events, traditions, ancestry, rituals past and modern. These and others, assisted by the appropriate diction, establish a context, the resonances of life. But these resonances, this orchestration they create, should not be like a garment that you can simply strip off. They are an organic part of your story and its people, its events.

If you invest everything in protest, then there must be little else that interests, you about the human condition in this part of the world. I mean especially the human condition that touches you immediately from your own environment. There will be nothing more to say when the political situation has changed, or when protest needs to be directed elsewhere. Hell,

Padi, there is a drama here that needs recording, replaying, recreating: people still make love, betray one another, knife or shoot one another down, father and son still love each other and also fight, a woman still sits by the roadside and suckles a baby in the summer or winter sun. If you are going to be a writer, and given your own powers of observation and our pain, you cannot in any way neglect the experience of the underdog, the victim of political tyranny. This is a given. You have to replay that experience in order to reveal, illuminate some aspect of it so that you help us discover other and more enduring meanings, beyond the pain of the instant. Or at least make us think and feel your exploration of the meanings.

It seemed, when my peers and I were being apprenticed each in his self-built and self-conducted workshop of the mind so to speak, that there must exist an easier method of learning how to write. Maybe you've come across the writings of Richard Rive, Alex la Guma, Bloke Modisane, Arthur Maimane, Bessie Head, Alfred Hutchinson, Lewis Nkosi, Can Themba, yes, no? Only Arthur, Lewis and I among them are still alive. They were my peers. We slugged it out the rough way. I remember vividly how bitter we all were, each in his/her own way. We knew everyone of us was choking on the heartburn. I poured out the bitter stuff on paper until I felt literally sick from the poison with which my adrenalin was flooding my veins. Something had to give. We all, except Rive, felt the compulsion to haul our arses out of the country.

So what am I saying? That it is a long painful process. Yet, not to obey the inner compulsion to write is to shrivel up slowly in your self-esteem. There was no one you could consistently consult and show work for a critical evaluation. I consulted Nadine Gordimer. She immediately took a liking for the short story "The Suitcase." A second didn't impress her.

From then on I was all on my own. I also say this to underscore the thick darkness in which we were operating in the fifties, let alone in the previous decades. You have workshops today we didn't create back then. Publishers are pounding at your door looking for manuscripts. Especially by unpublished writers. I'm green with envy for having been born too soon! I'm trying to impress upon you the need for you to exploit those experienced writers who are willing to help you — like myself. Badger them with your manuscripts.

Writing is a pleasurably painful business. It is most gratifying when a publisher has taken notice of what you've produced and will print it. But think also of literature as an act of culture, an act of language, and an act of self-knowledge. You see what a serious business it is? Your kind of revolution as a future writer consists in the revitalisation of experience, of language, of self, of our emotions and to increase us.

Go to it, and happy writing!

Zeke

29 Living with a paradox

Liz McGregor

IT IS the revelation that his son once French-kissed a black woman that worries Rian Malan's Afrikaner father. But it is from the left that Malan himself is braced for attack. "I expect to be vilified," he says with a grin. "It hasn't happened yet but I'm sure someone will gratify me sooner or later.'

It was his father's people, the Malan tribe — from Jacques Malan, a Huguenot who fled religious persecution in France in 1688 to the most notorious Malan of them all, General Magnus Malan, hawkish Defence Minister — that Rian Malan set out to pillory when he started the book that became My Traitor's Heart.

But his plot backfired. The Afrikaner socialist who sought to repudiate his roots now finds himself mired in African soil, groping for a centre to hold together his warring countrymen. "Journalism is effete," announces Rian Malan, aged 35, at the offices of his publishers in Pimlico, London. He is chain-smoking Silk Cut, lanky and elegant in mismatched charcoal suit and cotton jumper. An avid fisherman, his latest ambition is to farm barbel, African catfish to the uninitiated.

With typical self-deprecating humour, he recounts in his book how, as a 16-year-old radical anxious to prove his anti-apartheid bona fides, he lost his virginity to a domestic worker. "The next day at school I casually mentioned I had taken a black lover. My chinas [friends] were impressed. This was a truly staggering defiance of the rockspider [Afrikaner] tyranny. I sat there smiling modestly, praying no one would ask her name. I didn't know it, you see."

His father, reading this story, is afraid his brothers will be shocked. "But he is still talking to me," says Malan.

After a stint as crime reporter on the Johannesburg Star, he left South Africa in 1977 to avoid an army call-up or, as he sums it up in his book: "I ran away because I hated Afrikaners and loved blacks. I ran away because I was an Afrikaner and feared blacks. You could say, I suppose, that I ran away from the paradox."

After years of drifting he ended up in Los Angeles, writing rock and roll reviews under the name Nelson Mandela. Then, in 1985, came the news that South African townships were blowing apart. "South Africa was the top story on US TV that year. Publishers were throwing money at anyone who went there. I thought I'd look at three generations of Malans, white and Coloured."

His agent loved it. "He was touting it as a sort of Boer 'Roots'. A man from Hollywood even bought the rights to the mini-series." And so the exile returned. "They say that junkies sometimes put themselves through the cold sweats and sickness of withdrawal just so that they can start anew and experience that wild rush of intoxication for the first time," he explains in his book. "Coming home was like that."

He worked on the Malan dynasty for the first six to nine months, "based on the notion that I was an objective person standing outside the great South African drama; looking at my father and his brothers, saying how vicious they were."

Day after day he toiled through archives, researching his family's past "from the correct ideological perspective". "Then I'd fall asleep and have these dreams that were much more telling about what was going on in my psyche, what had always been there. They went right to the heart of what it was to be a white South African."

The Malan saga bit the dust. The rebel had found a better cause. Drawing on his experience as crime reporter he decided to explore his country through the medium of everyday South African murders: whites torturing a passing black to death over a Sunday afternoon braaivleis [barbecue]; the Zulu Hammerman who specialised in smashing sleeping white suburban heads; the UDF Comrades who burnt, stabbed and finally shot a 14-year-old Black Consciousness rival. It was this that was most likely to annoy the left. "My black Charterist [UDF] friends wanted me to remove that chapter," he says. "They tried to deny the very existence of black-on-black violence."

Malan had set out on his journey of discovery equipped with "the orthodox view: that the country was populated by caricature white villains and black heroes pitted against each other in classic Marxist class struggle." What he found was much less comforting: "I was living in a society held together largely by fear. And I was afraid too. But if you had the politics I was supposed to have, you were not allowed to have that fear.

"The truth was that I shat myself whenever I went into the townships. And I didn't know anyone who covered the townships who didn't have bad experiences simply because they were white. Alan Cowell of the New York Times, who was thrown out of South Africa because he was such a thorn in the side of the authorities, went into Alexandra one day. The Comrades saw a white skin and came out with petrol bombs. They blocked every exit and he drove round and round while they threw bricks the size of a man's head at him."

Malan believes that the 1985/86 township revolt was a turning point for South Africa: "It seemed to me that from 1986 onwards it had become an increasingly complex country and confusing for everyone who lived there. Before that, for the left it was very easy: you knew who everyone was and what they were doing wrong; the ANC spoke for the people. The ANC remains a formidable factor but I fail to see the ANC as the sole authentic representative of the masses in South Africa. The PAC guys are getting a lot of press; there are the BC guys, Inkatha. And the community councillors and others who work within the apartheid structures are not going to vanish, not without a struggle anyway.

"My book undermines traditional orthodoxy about South Africa but it was time for that orthodoxy to be undermined."

The only hope for South Africa, Malan believes, is a "just system", endorsed by all. "I don't see why you can't have Afrikaners of a certain ilk in a homeland of their own — and if a certain segment of Zulus want to live under Gatsha, let them. We will never have peace until we have a social contract to which everyone subscribes."

My Traitor's Heart, by Rian Malan is published by The Bodley Head.

30 A place not on the map

Ian Mayes

IF YOU drive about 35 miles towards the east from Bloemfontein, through the white farmlands and across the plains of the Orange Free State, you will come upon a place that does not appear on the map. It is revealed suddenly, just off the main road, a great straggle that has grown there in little over 10 years.

It used to be called Onverwacht, which in Afrikaans, means "unexpected". Today its new name is spelt out in stones on the low hills which rise to one side of it: Botshabelo. In the language of the South Sotho people it means "place of refuge". Social workers describe it more accurately as a dumping ground for blacks who are surplus to the requirements of the local economy.

This is a township — a city — of some 500,000 rural people, second in size only to Soweto but with practically none of the things which usually support communities on this scale. Made-up roads are spasmodic and peripheral. Brick built homes are few and mainly for employees of the government. Water is from taps which may mean a walk of half a mile. Little more than three per cent of homes have electricity, about two per cent have flush toilets and at a recent count, in the entire place there were 33 telephones. Transport is confined to the subsidised buses that take nearly 15,000 manual workers and domestic servants to and from Bloemfontein every day. Beyond that it hardly matters. No one is going anywhere.

What Botshabelo does have is huge unemployment — one report a year ago put it at 80 per cent — and it has hunger and all the diseases of poverty. "If you want to see a symbol of apartheid," a French doctor said, "then look no farther."

She was right. Botshabelo is a product of the complicated mess of the government's hated homelands policy. When Bophuthatswana was given its nominal independence at the end of the 1970s, one of the conditions was that it included an area around Thaba Nchu, traditionally occupied mainly by Tswana people.

It did and now this tiny enclave forms one of the seven separate parts of Bophuthatswana, ludicrously strung out across north-central South Africa, a geographical nonsense that a government minister once attempted to justify by comparing it to the Greek islands. Thaba Nchu has all the benefits of phoney independence: Kentucky Fried Chicken and a casino, where the local chief might be seen playing the one-armed bandits.

It also has one of the earliest surviving Wesleyan missions in the country, founded 150 years ago, by the Rev James Archbell, who was there in time to offer hospitality to the Voortrekkers, and who later, not to be outdone in enterprise, moved on to Natal, founded a bank, issued his own banknotes and became Mayor of Pietermaritzburg. In 1877, a decade after his death, his house at Thaba Nchu was visited, I was told by the present minister, "by your British MP, Anthony Trollope." Living here has given the Rev Eric Mahlatsi a glimpse of the apocalypse. He waved an arm to embrace, it seemed, the whole of South Africa. "A black and white civil war," he said, is "definitely coming."

The Methodist flock is now scattered, because when this part of Bophuthatswana came into being, it not only enclosed Tswana people, but in the kind of untidiness which the tidy system of the homelands creates, it also threw a cordon round thousands of Sotho people. They claimed harassment by the new Bophuthatswana administration, which had labelled them squatters, and following the example of Mr Archbell, they left.

They became the involuntary founders of Botshabelo, initially squatting on the white farm which gave the place its first name — a farm quickly acquired by the government in an attempt, it might have seemed, to contain the situation.

At the beginning of the 1980s there were 50,000 to 60,000 people in Botshabelo. Thousands more poured in as the abolition of the farm tenancy system and increasing mechanisation forced them off farms. At the same time, Bloemfontein restricted the growth of its own black township, and many of the smaller white towns in the province "disestablished" theirs. Botshabelo, the place of refuge, the "dump" for all these people, was thus the grim product of social engineering.

Then in December 1987, the government, setting earlier reassurances to one side, made its overall intention clear. It announced the incorporation of Bot-

A PLACE NOT ON THE MAP

shabelo into the tiny Sotho homeland of Qwa Qwa, more than 120 miles away on the other side of Lesotho. According to some reports, leaflets giving notice of incorporation were dropped on Botshabelo from security forces helicopters. The Chief Minister of Qwa Qwa, Kenneth Mopeli, said the people of Botshabelo danced in the streets in celebration of the news. Church observers said the scene was one of roadblocks, Casspirs of the South African Defence Force, and burning buses.

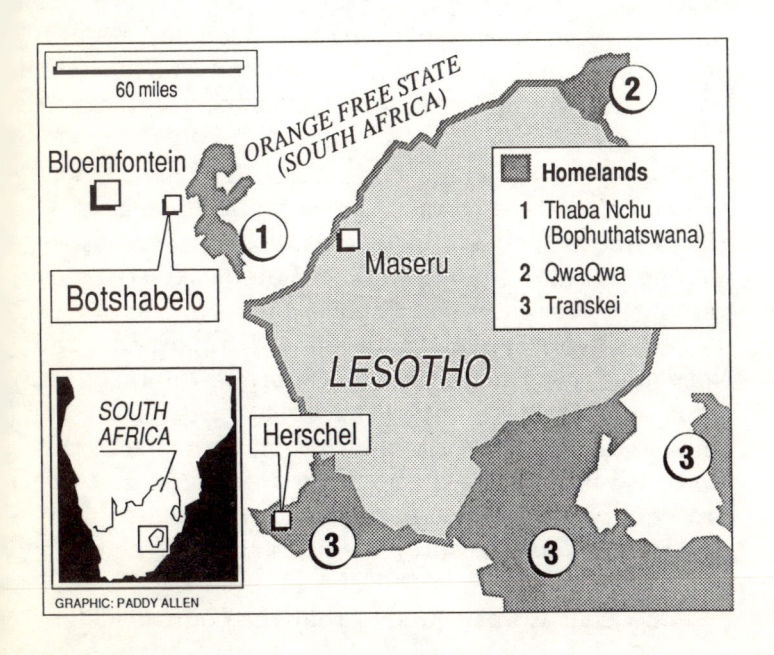

Since then there has been a long-running battle through the courts between the residents of Botshabelo, fighting to stay in South Africa, and the government, which plainly wants them out. The courts have supported the people. The Supreme Court in Bloemfontein declared the incorporation invalid, pointing out among other things that Botshabelo included some 120,000 "foreign blacks", non-Sotho people. Thus the kind of problem that had arisen in Bophuthatswana between the Tswanas and the Sothos could be repeated. The Appeal Court agreed with that decision.

The reasons for this long struggle, marked by petitions, marches and demonstrations, are not complicated. The people of Botshabelo fear that incorporation into Qwa Qwa would make their plight worse and, in the long run, disenfranchise them. The Chief Minister of Qwa Qwa wants them in because it would strengthen his own power and make the small homeland over which he reigns a more viable unit for the sort of independence Bophuthatswana has. And the South African government wants them out, because half a million black people, having been corralled in Botshabelo, in effect would be removed from the country altogether — it would be voting with their feet.

Since the Appeal Court ruling, the government has said it now accepts that Botshabelo is part of South Africa. The adminstration of Qwa Qwa says it no longer wants it. The people of Botshabelo still look nervously over their shoulders.

Joanne Yawitch, the co-ordinator for the National Land Committee, an umbrella organisation for a number of voluntary agencies involved in the homelands, says, "Walking through this place, this apartheid folly, a city without any infrastructure, you can't fail to become aware of all the complicated problems it poses for the future. What is going to become of all these people?"

She finds it unsurprising that the court decisions

have not dispelled the universal sense of insecurity. The government, she points out, has a history of enacting new legislation to get its way.

There are examples of government activity here: the two thousand or so neat bungalows that stand amid the "informal dwellings", the tin shanties and the mud huts. It has built supermarkets and schools. There is a small hospital and there are mobile clinics.

The government has now stopped building houses there but its agent, the South African Development Trust, in theory at least, is making sites available for people who want to build their own homes. The price has jumped dramatically. A site of 300 square metres used to cost 49 Rand. The price today is R60. The same site "with services" is R650 (£150) No one is quite sure what "with services" means, but the question is academic. The price is wildly beyond the means of most people living there. Around the approach to Botshabelo there is a cluster of 50 or so small factories making clothing and video equipment. Many of them are run by Taiwanese, a few by Israelis, recruited by government emissaries offering enormous subsidies which guarantee them virtually free labour. The government pays 95 per cent of the monthly wages for each worker up to a maximum of R100 (£23) for seven years.

In exchange for their labour, many workers earn less than a maid might get in the suburbs of Johannesburg. On occasions when they have tried to unionise they have been sacked. They are not difficult to replace. The South African Broadcasting Corporation once called this "a dynamic regional development programme".

Voluntary organisations make a small deduction

from the total misery. One of these is Operation Hunger, founded in 1980 when Botshabelo's explosive growth was already under way. Across the country this organisation feeds 1,300,000 people every day. It feeds 60,000 in the Orange Free State and Thaba Nchu, most of them in Botshabelo. Its founder and executive director, Ina Perlman, criticising the distribution of government funds for black development, says, "Not one project put forward has relevance to the people at the bottom of the heap, the black people in the rural areas." She believes that lessons should be drawn from the subsistence farming of the black peasant of the 19th century.

The pain of separation from the land is almost tangible in some of the people Operation Hunger helps in Botshabelo. Among them are the farmers from Herschel, now in the Transkei. They were promised, but then denied, land in Qwa Qwa. Now they live in tents and shacks in Botshabelo, believing that if they move out they will never get their land. There is a dogged cleanliness in this forlorn encampment. Hanging in one shack is a tea towel carrying "My Prayer". The first verse reads, "Bless my pretty kitchen Lord/ And light it with Thy love. Help me plan and cook my meals/ From Thy heavenly home above." Most of the meals are the maize porridge or fortified soup that Operation Hunger provides.

The leader of the Herschelites, Mr David Tseki, has a clip-board recording his long struggle with the authorities. At one time he was jailed. "Death was smelling in my nose," he told me. Seven hundred people came from Herschel. Many have drifted off into other parts of Botshabelo. Mr Tseki is surrounded by the faithful remnant.

A PLACE NOT ON THE MAP

Operation Hunger's co-ordinator for the Orange Free State, a 34-year-old Zimbabwean, Anthony Mfila, showed me some of the self-help projects he has organised. Dotted around the place are tiny workshops, women making dresses and children's clothes, men making furniture and chicken-wire fencing. Most sell their work for a greater return than the factories would provide.

The greatest investment is in small garden plots growing spinach and other vegetables. Some of these are irrigated in the long, dry season by water from a borehole sunk by Operation Hunger. On one of the days I was there, they were in danger of being washed away by heavy rain. The soil is poor and easily eroded. In wet weather Botshabelo quickly becomes a quagmire. An MP who visited the place last winter was unable to meet the people he had gone to see, because they were marooned by the mud. In one of the open cemeteries that stretch out across the grassland around Botshabelo, water cascading off the hills has formed deep runnels that threaten to expose the graves.

Anthony Mfila drove me back to the airport in Bloemfontein. On the way he pointed to land alongside the road. "That's where they plan to build the golf course," he said.

31 Accused One and Two

Alan Rusbridger

LIEUTENANT Lotz of the South African Police is not how you imagine your average torturer. He sits in a chunky woollen jumper at the side of Court 21, sometimes smiling quietly at the defence evidence, sometimes shaking his head, sometimes tweaking his neat blond moustache.

Three or four yards away sit Accused One and Two, the men he is said to have tortured. They slump back casually in blue track suits browsing through the early editions of the evening paper, glancing all around the court except at Lieutenant Lotz. At the back of the room, painted in municipal two-tone brown and cream gloss, are 50 or so Comrades, come to lend support and say goodbye. At the front are the white lawyers, the white sociologist, the white prosecutor and the white magistrate. It is a very South African scene.

Accused One and Two are guilty: the court has already ruled. Their confessions were thrown out earlier in the trial because of their claims (denied by

ACCUSED ONE AND TWO

Lieutenant Lotz) of torture. But the magistrate, Mr Lombard, relied heavily on the evidence of an anonymous ANC informer — Witness X — to convict them anyway. So all that is left to settle are the sentences.

A month or so ago, it would have been seven years and 10 years. But this is the new South Africa, and in the new South Africa there are few certainties.

It is time to give Accused One and Two the identities they are denied in Court 21. Accused One is Pule Sebidi, 29, from Pimville, Soweto. Two is Dumisane Nkabinde, 28, also from Pimville. The story of how Pule and Dumisane came to be in the dock in Court 21 of the Regional Division of Southern Transvaal in West Street, Johannesburg, is wholly unexceptional and, like many unexceptional things, more than usually interesting.

Pule is one of five children, Dumisane one of six. Pule's family had one room in his great grandmother's house in Pimville. Dumisane started life in a two-roomed tin shack nearby. Both have early and vivid memories of the small change of apartheid — being banned from the local ice rink; Pule seeing his father screamed at by a white manager.

But both Pule and Dumisane had ambitious parents who encouraged their education. At the time they first met — in their late teens — they were both doing well as students at Musi High School. Then they were hit by the mass resignation of teachers in 1977. White teachers moved into the schools. Some were good: others, they say, were rude, racist and lazy. Pule and Dumisane were expelled for being "troublemakers." They struggled on with their studies, but the new school they attended had few books, no facilities and big classes. Around the same time the Minister of

Bantu Education ordered that half the subjects in black high schools should be taught in Afrikaans. In the student protests that followed both Pule and Dumisane had friends and neighbours shot dead by police. Dumisane's brother was incarcerated for two years.

Both struggled on with their education: their parents struggled on with the fees. Dumisane was accepted for a BSc at Wits University in Johannesburg, but was refused a permit because the same course was available at a "tribal" university. Both ended up at the University of Zululand, at Ngoya where they set up the first branch of AZASO — a black political student union.

The main rival to AZASO on the campus was Chief Buthelezi's moderate — and widely despised — Inkatha movement. In the summer of 1984 there were student protests over a proposed visit by Buthelezi, who was chancellor of the university. The day before the visit police dispersed student gatherings with teargas and batons. Many students left the campus. Pule and Dumisane went further. They slipped across the border into Swaziland and made for an ANC military training camp.

In time both Pule and Dumisane trained with Mkhonto we Sizwe (MK), the military wing of the ANC, in Angola. In time Pule blew up a wall outside a military barracks with a limpet mine. In time they were identified by "Witness X." In time they came to make the acquaintance of Lieutenant Lotz. And in time they found themselves as Accused One and Two in Court 21 of the Southern Transvaal Regional Division, listening to pleas in mitigation by Dr Mark Orkin, the sociologist hired by the defence. Mr Orkin has seen both One and Two in prison and is impressed by their rationality and seriousness of purpose. He tells the court they acted with "moral authenticity." Their actions are, he says, an example of what the philosopher GH von Wright calls practical or moral syllogism. Lieutenant Lotz allows himself a quiet smile at his shoes. Up on the bench, Mr Lombard lets out a silent sigh.

Mr Orkin proceeds to underline the little ironies of the present case. Since the trial started back in October President De Klerk has unbanned the ANC and has committed the government to removing many of the injustices against which Accused One and Two fought.

Would prison deter them? But their kind of action would be unnecessary under the new South Africa. Would prison rehabilitate them? But how can one be rehabilitated from idealistic beliefs, which even the government now shares? Would prison punish them? But why punish people for their idealism in a climate of political reconciliation?

Mr Lombard wants a day or two to think it over. The Comrades at the back of the court break into chant. *Viva Mkhonto we Sizwe*. Accused One and Two gather up the two plastic bags containing their worldly goods and disappear down to the cells.

Friday, and we gather to hear Mr Lombard's thoughts. Though he shares English with the Accused, he chooses to deliver his judgment in Afrikaans, with an elderly interpreter at his side. Accused One and Two listen impassively, until the sentence is translated into Zulu, whereupon they break into gleaming grins. Deduct the suspended sentences and they've got off with one year and four years respectively. A few months ago it would have been seven and 10. Down in the cells, Pule is delighted. Four years on Robben Island is just what he needs to complete his accountancy and business economics course. Dumisane hopes to spend the time working on his maths.

But the unspoken question in Court 21 is the most basic one: what lies four years, or even one year, down the road to the new South Africa? Will Pule Sebide really end up a chartered accountant? And Dumisane Nkabinde a physicist? And what, then, of Lieutenant Lotz?

Contributors

David Beresford has been the Guardian's correspondent in South Africa since 1985. He previously served as an Assistant Foreign Editor in London and has also reported extensively from Northern Ireland. He is author of Ten Men Dead, an analysis of the prison hunger strikes in Northern Ireland in 1981.

Michael Billington has been Drama Critic of the Guardian since 1971 and has worked as the London Arts Correspondent of the New York Times since 1978. He frequently broadcasts on radio and television and is the author of studies of Alan Ayckbourn, Tom Stoppard and Peggy Ashcroft.

Breyten Breytenbach emigrated to Europe from South Africa in 1959 and campaigned actively against apartheid. He returned secretly in 1975 and was sentenced to nine years in prison for "terrorism". He served seven years before his release in 1982. He now lives in Paris. His most recent book, All One Horse: Fictions and Images, is published by Faber.

Alex Brummer is the Guardian's Financial Editor and has written extensively on international economic, financial, development and aid issues. From 1979-89 he was the paper's Washington Correspondent. He was named best Foreign Correspondent in the US by the Overseas Press Club in 1989.

Georgina Henry is the Guardian's Media Editor. She joined the newspaper in February 1989.

Angella Johnson has been a reporter on the Guardian for two years. A graduate of the City University School of Journalism in London, she was previously a reporter on the Times and the London Daily News.

Frank Keating has been a sports columnist with the Guardian since 1976, in which capacity he has won numerous awards. He is the author of nine books and is a regular broadcaster.

Liz McGregor works on the Guardian arts desk. She grew up in South Africa and worked on local papers, including the Rand Daily Mail and Cape Times, for seven years before leaving for Britain in 1985.

Nomavenda Mathiane is Assistant Editor of Frontline, an independent monthly political magazine started in 1979. It has three staff and a circulation of 10,000. Frontline has just lost an appeal against R12,000 damages and costs in a libel action taken by the Inkatha president, Chief Mangosuthu Buthelezi.

Ian Mayes is Deputy Features Editor of the Guardian. He edited (with Margaret Busby) an Africa issue of Weekend Guardian which included contributions from Chinua Achebe, Nuruddin Farah, Ngũgĩ wa Thiong'o, Ben Okri, Wole Soyinka, and the exiled South African writers, Breyten Breytenbach and Lewis Nkosi. He was previously Assistant Features Editor of the London Daily News.

Douglas Morrison, a senior member of the Guardian features department staff, began his newspaper career in South Africa. Before joining the Guardian he was Chief Sub-Editor of the Times Higher Education Supplement.

Es'kia Mphahlele was born in Marabastad, a township of Pretoria, in December 1919. His first volume of autobiography, Down Second Avenue, was published at the end of the 1950s while he was in Nigeria at the beginning of nearly 20 years of exile which also took him to Europe and the United States. He returned to South Africa in 1977. His literary output includes novels, short stories, poetry and essays. He is the director of the Council for Black Education.

Roger Omond, Chief Foreign Sub-Editor of the Guardian, is the author of The Apartheid Handbook, Steve Biko And Apartheid, and co-author of The Sanctions Handbook. He worked as a journalist in South Africa until 1978 when he came to Britain. He has been awarded the Guardian Nuffield Research Fellowship for 1990.

Judy Rumbold is the Guardian's Style Editor. After graduating from St Martin's School of Art in London she worked at the Institute of Contemporary Arts and the Sunday Times before joining the Guardian in 1987.

Alan Rusbridger is the Guardian's Features Editor. Previously he edited the Guardian Diary, was a feature writer and columnist on the Observer and worked as Washington Correspondent for the London Daily News.

Hugo Young has been the Guardian's Chief Political Columnist since 1984. Before that he was successively Political Editor and Deputy Editor of the Sunday Times. He was nominated Columnist of the Year three times in the British Press Awards and once by Granada Television's What The Papers Say judges. He is the author of seven books, including One Of Us, a highly acclaimed assessment of the first 10 years of the Thatcher government.

Acknowledgements

Thanks to: Lindsay Fort, Justus de Goede, Paul Howlett, Ingrid Hudson, Rosemarie Hunter, Mike Kantey, Norma Lancaster, Patrick Laurence, Elnor and John Leach, John Leask, Anne McHardy, Jim McKinney, Tony Morphet, Louis Mullinder, Mark Orkin, Ken Parker, John Patterson, David Philip, Benjamin Pogrund, Jenny Pogrund, John Rees, Noel Stott, Barry Streek, Rob Turrell, David Watts, Brian Whitaker.